The Invisible Woman Becomes Visible!

• • • ◆ ◆ ◆ ◆ ◆ • • •

A CHRISTIAN'S JOURNEY THROUGH
CORPORATE AMERICA

GWENDOLYN J. WHEELER

Fulton Books, Inc.
Meadville, PA

Published by Fulton Books 2021

ISBN 978-1-63710-806-2 (paperback)
ISBN 978-1-63710-807-9 (digital)

Printed in the United States of America

This book is dedicated to the memory of my friend, Penny T. She was one of my companions who did not fare well in corporate America. We stayed in touch even after we started working at different companies.

Sadly, I wish we could have had one more phone call or dinner together. I got busy, and I regret that. Benjamin Franklin said, "Don't put off until tomorrow what you can do today." When I finally called her to wish her a Merry Christmas, the woman who answered the phone at her job asked who I was. I said I was a friend. She told me Penny T. was deceased. The pain of those words is indescribable.

That woman probably thought to herself, "What kind of friend doesn't know her friend died?" Her brother had a private service. None of her friends were invited. She died alone in her apartment from natural causes.

Living with regrets does not change the fact that painful event occurred. I had to stop feeling guilty that I allowed life to get in my way, which prevented me from seeing my friend. There had to be a plan in place to keep me from being stuck in a place called regrets over what I should have done. My plan was to remember the time we spent together. During our time together we laughed, we cried, and we plotted ways to survive the corporate drama. Our united front preserved our sanity as we dealt with some of the managerial shenanigans. I will always remember you, my friend. You are a corporate champion!

CONTENTS

INTRODUCTION

· · ◆ ● ● ◆ ● ● ◆ · ·

After spending thirty-seven years in corporate America, I couldn't leave without writing a dramatic final farewell. I started my writing about this journey in 2005 in my second book, *On the Road to Recovery Again*. Chapter 13 was entitled "Recovering from Corporate Drama." The story of my thirty-plus years in corporate America was not completed in that book. I was still at a company where there were lessons I had learned but could not publicly publish them. Now that I am officially retired from corporate America, I can finish my story.

The names of the companies that I worked at and their employees have been changed. If there are stories and characters that sound familiar, you may be one of the leading actors. On the other hand, it might not be you at all. Maybe it is one of your cousins, who graduated from the same school of self-importance that you graduated from.

Roles, stories, and roads of corporate life at times cross paths. You can hear so many within its hollow halls screaming, "This cannot be happening again!" They thought they would not have to encounter that experience again.

This is my attempt, like an artist, to put my finishing touches on the canvas of my journey as a Christian through corporate America. I emphasize Christian because I had to be reminded constantly to conduct myself in a Godly manner when I felt I was being treated unfairly. In the 1990s, the phrase "What would Jesus do?" began. That phrase was a reminder for Christians to attempt to act in a way that personified Jesus's teachings from the Gospels. Admittedly, I failed a lot. Too many times I reacted in a manner that did not personify the Gospel. In hindsight, I would have loved to have been the perfect Christian and handled things differently. Frankly, some of the events encountered were very challenging.

Yet those experiences left me enriched and not diminished. Many lessons were learned, and I became stronger. Unique gifts were discovered within, and I brought them proudly to the table of life. When I was knocked down, I learned to be resilient and combated the lies with truth—telling the truth and living it.

Further, I rose up and grew into this incredibly beautiful, intelligent, creative, strong, excellent, and amazing visible woman. I came of age. I grew up and took the power back from the perpetrators, who once made me feel invisible within the corporate arena. This once invisible woman emerged into visibility.

The title of this book will be explained in the first chapter, so keep reading.

Chapter 1

· · ◆ ◆ ◆ ◆ ◆ · · ·

The Invisible Woman Becomes Visible!

How to Successfully Overcome the Invisible Syndrome

The name of this book was derived from a college course, Systems Theory of Psychology. By the way, I received an A in that course. The professor said, "You deserved it." One of the major lessons I learned was, when people don't value you, they can make you invisible. That feeling of being made invisible is what we will call the invisible syndrome. The word *value* means worth, importance, usefulness, appreciation, respect, and esteem. If anyone has ever tried to make you feel less than valuable, then they were treating you like you were invisible. That psychology class became my therapy and helped me to understand the frustrations I experienced while walking through the hollow halls of corporate America.

Too often that treatment is flagrant or unconcealed throughout the corporate arena. The invisible syndrome can be perpetuated in so many different ways. To illustrate this truth, stories are shared that show examples of the invisible syndrome. Identities as indicated in the introduction have been concealed. Sometimes it feels like I am writing my first novel, but this is nonfiction. These events actually occurred.

Every journey has a beginning. Too many people start out not knowing where they are going—no real purpose or dreams are in view. Sometimes a journey is created by a present need that we want to satisfy. For an eighteen-year-old senior in high school, my corporate journey began early because the money was limited in the Wheelers' household. My father died when I was fifteen years old, and my mother's LPN salary was not enough to cover all the living expenses. She did her best, and I wanted to be one less person she had to take care of. Financial independence was a priority for me even then.

My school guidance counselor didn't encourage me to go to college. In that era, minority students weren't generally advised to go to college. Getting a job immediately after graduation made sense to me. My minority friends and schoolmates, who rose above what was expected of them and achieved a college education, are applauded. The word *college* is italicized because we all receive an education, whether it is through formal education or education in corporate or other arenas. I did take college courses, seminars, and workshops but did not complete a formal degree program yet. Instead, I received a corporate education, and I am a life coach professor who can teach and advise others on how to navigate through the hollow halls of corporate America.

During my senior year of high school, I started working part-time as a mail clerk at a local bank. Starting in the mail room did not make me happy, but that was where the bank started the young and inexperienced. My time in the mail room was only for a short time, and then I was moved over into the banking business area. The minimum wage back then was about $1.39 per hour. It was spending money for me.

After I graduated from high school, I worked for a couple of insurance companies, but I am going to fast-forward and talk about my experience with a company we will call Water Storage Company. My career at this company spanned approximately fourteen years. Cheers and tears were experienced during my employment. When I started there, I was a nineteen-year-old, naive, young woman.

Upon my departure, I was a mature, confident thirty-three-year-old woman.

The stories at this company are woven throughout the rest of this book. Therefore, you will not be able to trace my journey chronologically. This book is purposely written in a jigsaw puzzle form that cannot easily be put back together. You have to guess where I am and when I was there. The lessons learned are the purpose of this book. As the old hymn goes, "If I can help somebody as I travel along, then my living shall not be in vain." I want to help, encourage, and hopefully restore some sanity to the corporate travelers.

The corporate experience is not a well-manicured journey. There are some straight paths, twist, turns, potholes, valleys, mountains, obstacles, detours, roadblocks, delays, stress, betrayals, dream busters, dead-end streets, joys, laughter, promotions, training, friendships, heartaches, loneliness, encouragement, mentors, and many changes. Every journey isn't the same, and yours may not be as colorful as mine has been.

Most of my thirty-seven-year corporate journey was spent in a secretarial/administrative role. This book is separated according to experiences. When possible I will give it a name, not the real name of course.

Water Storage Company (WSC)

At the beginning of my journey, administrative persons were treated like their boss's property. One day a customer asked me if I was my boss's girl. I said rather proudly and defiantly, "I am his secretary." The elderly gentleman replied, "You are his girl then!" That remark made me feel invisible. Being a person of color, I felt like he was telling me that I was my boss's slave. I didn't like that.

Later, when a new sales director, Sergio, was placed over our sales field office, he perpetuated the invisible syndrome. He was determined to make changes that would reflect his personality. This was my first encounter with male chauvinism in the workplace. Lois, the senior secretary, was openly Miss Women's Liberation. The two personalities collided very quickly. Sergio told Lois he wanted her to sense when he needed her. If we didn't pick up things out of his outbox quickly enough, we were reprimanded.

One of the new policies Sergio instituted infuriated us. Lois and I had to bring coffee to any of the salespeople who wanted it. Women's rights were pushed back considerably. When I asked Wyatt if he wanted me to bring him coffee in the morning, he said, "If I want coffee, I'll get it myself." We loved his response. We applauded him.

Sergio treated Lois and I like we were invisible, but Lois got the worst of the deal. He put her on probation. Before he could execute his plan to fire her, he was promoted and transferred to the New York office. Thank God! Lois wrote me a note on a Post-it telling me Sergio was going to New York. I can still see that big smile on her face. Our prayers were answered. We celebrated, and the coffee service ended with his departure.

Arnold became the new director and took Lois off probation. We both liked him a lot.

I can still see that condescending smile that Sergio used to flaunt. He was self-absorbed. Years later I heard that he tried to get a younger secretary to buy theater tickets for him and his wife. She told him "no." In fact, I think she told him to have his wife go buy the tickets. At that point in history, women's rights now had to be respected. A new breed of secretaries entered the workplace saying, "We don't do coffee, buy gifts for wives/girlfriends, type college papers for your spoiled children, or any other personal thing." We cheered her on, and Human Resources supported her right to say no.

As I see it, I had one of the best seats in the house. While supporting the senior leaders of companies, I learned a lot from organizing their desks, the letters I typed, the papers I filed, the phone messages I took, the emails I read, and the conversations I overheard. Moreover, I observed how they treated their subordinates and the two faces that subordinates sometimes wore. They smiled in their boss's face but criticized them when they weren't around. You see, I was not only the boss's listening ear but the subordinates' listening ear. Yes, I could have told them their boy or girl didn't have their backs 100 percent, but they were so arrogant and full of themselves. Therefore, I knew the boss wouldn't believe me. When they promoted the subordinates and gave them raving reviews, I just shook my head. Great discipline was shown by not singing a rendition of "Smile in your face while stabbing you in the back."

Sooner or later life will educate you because people's true colors will come out. Corporate honeymoons eventually turn into corporate divorces. The definition for a corporate honeymoon is priceless, a short period of harmony or goodwill at the beginning of a relationship, especially in politics or business.

When Paul and Cindy first started working together, they seemed to be the perfect boss and subordinate couple. They were inseparable, going to lunch together and laughing like teenage lovers. It seemed like they were both united successfully against us. My partner in crime, Penny T., and I saw them in a different light. We knew it would only be a matter of time before their egos would collide. They would soon be at each other's throats. One afternoon we heard Paul saying to Cindy behind closed doors, "You are not going to get my job!" The honeymoon was over!

Stabbing folks in the back was a poisonous trait Cindy tried to get others to emulate. One day she tried to get me to turn on Penny T., but I wasn't desperate to climb the corporate ladder. Certainly I wasn't going to climb it at the expense of a friend. Besides, we were in a daily combat with her, and we needed to remain a united force. I have visions of how she would give us documents to type with the word *now* circled on the top. That was her way of saying I want you to drop everything and work on this project. There was a problem with that system: everything she gave us had *now* circled at the top. The obvious question was which is *now* number 1. People who are exploding with a false sense of self-importance are just insane, so don't expect anything they do or say to make sense.

There were some funny moments. Like the day I had taken a medication that had been recalled. Cindy jokingly said I had died. I told Penny T. I must be in hell if she was here with me.

Cindy's career at Water Storage Company ended abruptly. She recommended to the senior leadership to give low raises across the board to everyone in the company. That turned out to be an unwise decision. The promising young sales executives that WSC had spent so much money and time training started leaving. Our clients recognized those young soldiers' potential and scooped them up fast. Senior leadership used her as the scapegoat and told her to leave. I say that because she had to have their approval before she could implement that new company policy. They took her advice because she said a survey said those were the proper percentages. Her plan backfired. For the record, she had no prior experience working with salespeople. The sales force is the one who sold the products and brought revenue into the company for the rest of us. They expected to be properly compensated.

Cindy moved out of town and left the new house she built behind. It is scary, but I can still see that fake smile and the black hat she wore.

Another gentleman we will call Frank perpetuated my feelings of invisibility. One day Frank gave work to Lois, and she asked him about it. Right in front of me, he said, "You can give it to Gwen." I knew she was attending college at night and worked on homework during work hours. That was the day I was ready to say something to both of them because I felt I was doing my share of work. She wasn't any better than me. Thankfully she didn't give it to me. My reaction would have probably been the end of my career at that company. Write this note to yourself: It is always better to walk away, get a breath of fresh air if possible, and come back before you respond. Don't let your emotions control you or sabotage your career. A lot of things you experience in the corporate arena is temporary and will change quicker than you expect.

To add to my feelings of invisibility, we were expected to do personal things for our bosses and their families. Frank abused that unwritten rule. I had to type letters requesting contributions for his son's soccer team and political contributions for his political candidate. One time I had to type his son's college term papers, and his wife had the nerve to call me and tell me which one was due first. He gave me this as though it was part of my job description.

Even though my desk was full of company-related work, I was expected to make his personal requests a priority. I was understandably upset, but at that time I didn't feel I could say no without receiving repercussion from upper management.

Eventually change came to this small field office. Lois graduated from college and accepted a new job at a different company. Before she left, she attempted an invisibility act of betrayal. She tried to get the new director to hire her friend for her old position. Arnold surprised her and told her that position was going to be given to me. This was my first promotion in corporate America. The junior secretary/receptionist became the senior secretary. Today I would have been called the office manager, but those titles didn't exist back then. The extra responsibilities were just expected of you. My job description required me to do the following:

- Supervise the junior secretary.
- Manage and distribute the work assignments given to us by the nine salespeople.
- Order regular and coffee supplies.
- Keep the office organized.
- Manage postage machine and get refilled by going to post office.
- Manage calendars.
- Answer phones, which required you sometimes to diplomatically keep from telling customers that your boss was out playing golf or wasn't taking phone calls. As a Christian, you had to find a diplomatic way of not lying but not telling clients the truth either.
- Reconcile expense reports and reimburse salespeople by generating checks.
- Monitor money in checking account, which was used to reimburse salespeople for their expenses and pay for other office expenses. This required me to reconcile the check book and send proper form to corporate office to get money to replenish the office account.

Happily, the invisible syndrome seemed to be lifting, and I had now become visible.

Subsequently, as one writer wrote, "Change is inevitable. Change is constant." Our field office moved out to an industrial park, where public transportation was not available. Clearly, I wasn't an important factor in making this decision. This was convenient for all the salespeople who had cars. I did not have one. I loved my job, so I bought a car so I could make this move. Unfortunately, I purchased a car that was given a bad rating by *Consumer Report*, and other people I know advised me not to buy. Yet I thought it was cute. As warned by *Consumer Report*, the engine failed. I had to buy two cars in less than a year. In addition, the traveling expenses were getting the best of me. One day I even had to borrow money from my boss. That was a very humiliating experience for me, but I was broke.

By the way, the salespeople were reimbursed for their travel expenses to the office. I was not reimbursed for my travel, nor was my salary increased because of this additional expense. Regrettably, I did not think through all the factors thoroughly before making the decision to make this move. My broke self decided to find another job closer to home. Arnold said, "I hate to lose you!" Underline his response because later you will hear about a contradiction he wrote to that statement.

However, let's celebrate his initial support for my dilemma. He spoke to Michael in what was then called Personnel Department at our Boston location. They transferred me to a temporary position in Personnel. Michael was very nice and wrote a great evaluation before he left the company. He wrote, "She works well in difficult situations."

Generally, coming to the Boston office was a whole new world for me. The sales field office was a small office with a casual atmosphere. Transferring to the Boston office was like a country girl coming to the big city. It was corporate America in its entire splendor. I had to buy new clothes so that I could fit in. At first I floated between departments, and then the opportunity came for another promotion, but not without controversy.

At that time, my former boss, Arnold, was promoted and transferred to Boston. He needed an administrative person, and I was his obvious choice. When asked by him to work for him, I was excited about getting this new position, which involved working for a previous boss I really liked. Unfortunately, I wasn't aware of office politics and didn't know this wasn't a done deal. I learned a painful lesson about why you shouldn't tell the office gossip unofficial information. In my excitement, I told Ruby that I was going to be promoted and work for Arnold. She told others in the office. One of the women, Evelyn, wanted that position. Evelyn had more seniority in the company and experience in the area of customer service. The position was given to her, and Arnold told me about it as though that position was not verbally promised to me.

By that time, corporate America had really matured me, and Ms. Gwen was more outspoken. Understandably, I was upset about how this turned out but decided not to fight for the position. Instead, I wanted to leave it on record that I knew what actually happened. The person I chose to be my voice to management was Jerry, who was the controller. At first he tried to give a rehearsed managerial explanation. Then I told him in detail what had occurred. He smiled and said, "They didn't handle it right."

Some days later, Paul, the senior personnel manager, came and found me. He said to me, "You have been a real trooper, and we would like to offer you another position." His further words offered good corporate advice for anyone promised a promotion, "Don't tell anyone about this until it is finalized." I told him he didn't have to worry, because I had learned the hard way about talking about something before it was finalized. The new position was higher, more prestigious than the previous one they had offered. What is more, an office came with it. The personnel secretary was retiring, and they offered that position to me.

As a Christian woman, I knew this wasn't mere luck. Instead it was Romans 8:28 personified, which declares, "And we know that all things work together for good to those who love God, to those who are the called according to His purpose."

When my promotion was announced through the personnel employee communication bulletin, Personnel Announcement, I had a sense of great satisfaction and a feeling of sweet victory. More emphasis was placed on this promotion than the other woman's promotion. The looks of surprise on those ladies' faces were priceless. Now gossip about me behind my back with that news. The smirks that once occupied their faces after I didn't get the last position were gone. Signed, sealed, and delivered, the job was mine. It could not be taken away from me this time. There was a legal document in place. Arnold came into my office and congratulated me. I don't think the woman who got the other position working for him congratulated me.

In my new position, I supported two senior vice presidents and two senior managers. The secretary I replaced didn't believe in filing. Rumor was it was not her decision to retire, so she certainly wasn't going to tidy up the office for me. There were piles of paper everywhere. Paul came into my office one day and looked around at all the piles of papers and said to me, "I am sure you know this has got to go." With my strong organizational skills, I was able to clean that office up in a short period of time.

Unfortunately, my clean-up-the-office project uncovered a painful discovery. I told you earlier about how when I had to leave the sales office that Arnold said, "I hate to lose you!" Then I told you to underline his response because later you will hear about a contradiction he wrote to that statement. Here it is: Arnold wrote a performance evaluation about me that I never read or signed. He always told me verbally that I was doing a great job, but on this evaluation he listed negative things that I needed to improve on. My heart was broken. I was hurt and angry. How can you improve your work performance if you are not told you need to improve? Another fact, he could have increased my salary to keep me there. Clearly, I wasn't valuable. That evaluation was not properly noted. In fact, who could find anything in the piles of things on the desk and cabinets? Now I understood why God didn't allow me to work for him again. He could not be trusted to be honest. This position was more interesting and paid more.

After I cleaned and organized my new office, Paul came in and complimented me on how nice it looked. Shortly after that, I moved into a smaller office so that a new personnel manager could have the bigger office. My new office was a shared office separated by a wall.

This space was shared with Penny T. I made sure the movers put my desk in the middle of the work area so they could not later squeeze anyone else in there beside me. They were not taking this private space away from me.

Unfortunately, more surprises were to be uncovered. While looking through the salary file, I found out that they were paying the woman who replaced me as senior secretary in the field sales office the same amount they were paying me. My position was higher, and I had more seniority. Clearly, seniority and promotion only matters when management wants it to matter. Management in corporate America does whatever they want to do. The rules keep changing to justify whatever they want to do at any particular moment. Understandably, I became angry over this injustice. Then I heard the voice of God saying, "You cannot measure my blessing in dollars and cents." That gave perspective, and I calmed down. After Arnold's divorce, he started dating this woman. Do you think her higher salary had anything to with this relationship?

Incidentally, my time in Personnel didn't last very long. Paul and I started bumping heads a lot. Frankly, he was really annoying, so I requested a transfer into the Sales Leadership Department, and I kept two of the managers I was working for. Paul asked me if I was leaving because of him. I just looked at him, and that conversation was over.

Disappointingly, I experienced more of the invisible syndrome in the Sales Leadership Department. People try and make other people feel invisible for various reasons. They may be jealous or intimidated by another person's success. A woman we will call Mary tried to make me feel invisible because my bosses liked me so much. They thought I was wonderful and a lot easier to work with than Mary. On special occasions like Christmas and Secretaries' Day, they showered me with compliments, gifts, and flowers. Their appreciation of me ignited jealousy within her. I never could understand why because she had a higher position, made more money, dressed better than me, and was married to a man who absolutely adored and spoiled her.

However, she was still catty and sarcastic. Maybe she wanted to be the only one in the limelight. One day I heard her making a remark about the flowers my bosses had given me for Secretaries' Day. She said, "Her desk looks like a funeral." Another time I jumped when someone had almost bumped into me coming around the corner. I heard her say, "Jumpy, isn't she?" One of my bosses, Rudy, heard her remark and came to my defense. He said to Mary, "Are you having a bad day?" Rudy was glad I was his assistant and didn't have a problem making that fact known. He was a difficult person to work for, but I liked him a lot and was sad when he left.

Moreover, the evaluation system in place in that department was unfair. Mary was the administrative supervisor but really did not supervise me. I worked directly with my managers and vice presidents. We had to coordinate our time with her but received no input on how to do our jobs. Frankly I think they made up that position to make her feel she was promoted. Mary wrote my evaluation without any input from my bosses. She discounted the good things my bosses said about me. Through her written words, she tried to make me feel incompetent (invisible). When I questioned her about a remark she made, she could not give me an acceptable explanation. I guess she didn't expect me to question her, but I did. The salary increases given were small, and she definitely wasn't going to fight for me to get any more.

At the age of thirty-three, I came to the conclusion I wasn't going to advance or make too much money at Water Storage Company. The system in place prevented that. I decided I was too young to be stuck in a dead-end job that allowed me to be blocked by someone who constantly tried to make me feel less than who I was. Also, the cap they had placed on yearly salaries helped me to decide it was time to make a change.

When I found another job, Mary had the audacity to ask me what I was going to be making. I told her $5,000 more a year. That was $2,000 more than I asked for. She also said she didn't blame me for leaving. I don't think she realized that she was one of the main reasons I decided to leave. Now she could freely shine. The employees at WSC were shocked that I was leaving after almost fourteen years. Most employees retired from that company, but I could not picture myself staying there until retirement. I deserved to be treated better and to have more. This hardworking woman was determined to be visible.

InfoData Company

When I started working at a company we will call InfoData, I was so excited and was especially glad about the fact that I reported directly to my bosses. The primary person who hired me told me during the interview that they thought they had the person for this job but I upset the apple cart. Now that's a visibility comment. There was no in-between person to block my progress.

For the most part, my experience at this company was great. At the beginning, my evaluations and salary increases were excellent. It felt wonderful getting 12 percent salary increases. Eventually I asked for more responsibility and an opportunity for advancement. Management agreed, and training was put in place to develop me into an assistant account manager in our International Sales Department.

Then the unexpected occurred, a new sales director was hired. Jack Moses was young, arrogant, and insensitive. Everyone in the sales department had to meet with him and tell him our goals. He listened, and I thought he understood that I had trained well and was ready for advancement. I had handled increased responsibilities well. During the interim when they were waiting for new sales personnel to be hired, I was able to successfully collect about $60,000 from a couple of international customers. Management applauded me.

However, those success stories occurred before Jack arrived. He couldn't care less about the two years of professional sales training I received, which included hands-on training. The hard work I had put in was not acknowledged nor appreciated. In fact, when he called me back for a follow-up meeting, he coldly stated, "I know what you said you wanted to do, but your primary job will be to answer the Sales 800 line." He wasn't interested in my career goals. He wanted what he wanted and thought I should quietly go along with his plan. Again, I was made to feel invisible.

Frankly, going with the flow was not my intentions. Instead, I planned to fight this all the way. He just arrived at the company, and I had been there for seven years. It was not fair for him to expect me willingly to regress back into a straight administrative role. Thinking I was going to be content with answering phones and other administrative tasks was absurd. How dare he just expect me to forget about what I had been working so hard to achieve. I fought with everything within me to get what I wanted, but to no avail.

In fact, I went to our Human Resources representative and explained to her my situation. When she met with me again, she was telling me what Jack wanted me to do. Hello! You are not telling me anything I don't know. It was obvious she was going to support management and was not going to jeopardize her position for me. She didn't have to worry about me asking her for help anymore.

There was much tension between Jack and me. To make matters worse, he was the worst letter writer, speller, and unorganized person I ever met in my corporate life. I was expected to edit his letters and make him sound intelligent. Behind his back, people jokingly called his office the black hole. Things would get lost in there.

When an assistant account manager (AAM) position became available, Jack offered it to a young lady we will call Vickie, who did not have any sales experience. She began in the marketing department as an administrative assistant but was allowed to advance. After a few drinks at a cookout, she told me this information but said she turned it down. I was furious. It was obvious that he changed the rules whenever he wanted to or just had lied to me. He told me he wasn't hiring anybody for AAM positions unless they had previous selling experience. What further infuriated me was the fact that Vickie said he had problems with minorities. He had made a comment that a particular ethnic group was lazy. Vickie's roommate was from that particular ethnic group, so she defended her. After that night, I wondered if I had been a different color, would he have promoted me. I did not pursue the issue.

Sometime after that night, I confronted Jack about what Vickie said about him offering the position to her. He looked at me like I had two heads but did not deny it. He later eliminated the AAM position from the division. He probably reopened that position after I left the company. Yes, I know how that works.

In fairness to the international sales director, I kept doing the work of an AAM. I liked the client contact work.

The same psychology class that taught me about the invisible syndrome also taught me that we need to teach people what we want and then in turn listen to what they want. I met with Jack to teach him what I wanted and then listened to what he wanted. This time I came with a document of what I had achieved, and my request was different. I asked only for a title change from administrative assistant to sales coordinator. Just wanted validation and recognition of the contribution I made that didn't fall into the administrative assistant category.

Jack made a verbal agreement with me. Notice I said verbal agreement. He was careful not to put this in writing. Was his plan to reject my request from the beginning? Or did he underestimate my ability to achievé what he asked of me? I don't know. He told me what he wanted, and we agreed on a plan that would be reviewed in forty-five days. At his request, I went to each of his staff and asked how I could more effectively help them do their jobs. That was really humiliating for me because I had outgrown having to do stuff like that. It was like I had to take steps backward in order to go forward. Everybody was happy with me, but Jack didn't honor his agreement.

Shortly after that meeting, he was promoted to vice president and hired a new sales director. Jack gave her the task of making me feel invisible, and she denied the request of changing my title in writing. What a coward! I tried to get her to understand my needs, but she was interested in pursuing her own career goals. That meant she wasn't going to help me. They seemed to have a problem with the fact that I was taking college classes, and his denial was his way of telling me he was the one with the real power.

This new director we will call Clara. Clara was new to the game, and her plan of how she would succeed in her new position. That plan required giving me more nonadministrative responsibilities such as keeping track of the sales quota being achieved by each account manager. That would require me sharpening my skills to use the Excel software. In my most diplomatic way without being rude, I refused what she wanted under the excuse of "I don't know how to do that." Sorry. I needed more Jesus at that point. She had the nerve to complain to one of the new female account managers about me. I gave that new account manager an earful. It is an unreasonable expectation to expect someone to take on something new when you refuse to reward them for what they already have done. Since they wanted to treat me like I was invisible, I was going to be invisible to her request of taking on more responsibility.

I went through depression, and everyone chose to ignore my depression. They just didn't care. Then I got better. Jack actually seemed to become hostile and mad because I recovered from my depression. He probably was hoping that I would quit. The tension had grown thick again between us. We moved into a new office building, and my cubicle was located in a dark area, where an exit sign was located. Every morning I came to work, it felt like I was being shown the door. That was truly a prophetical sign.

One of my support system during this painful time was the program I was enrolled in at college. It was geared toward helping adults make career transitions. We got together in groups and talked about the problems we encountered within the workplace. Jack was always at the top of my discussions. One day a professor told us that there should always be a learning process in everything we do. I decided to tell my story about supporting an international sales force of fourteen people without appreciation and recognition. Then I asked the question, "What am I to learn from this?" The professor said, "You may have to learn it is time to look for another job." That was a prophetical statement. My fellow students were supportive. At one point I did feel like quitting, but two older women said to me, "Don't quit your job." I felt they were the voices of God.

One day Jack yelled at me from his office and asked if I had mailed a certain package to Europe last night. I said "no." He said, "I wanted you to." I yelled back, without leaving my cubicle or getting out of my chair, "Well, I didn't know." He thought he had indicated a time, but he didn't. Later that night when I was out to dinner with my sister, I said, "You know what? He yelled at me today, and I yelled back without even thinking about it or getting out of my chair." I laughed. It just didn't matter anymore. That man had just pushed me that far.

Shortly after that incident, my invisibility at InfoData ended. One afternoon around four o'clock, Jack left a Post-it note on my chair requesting that I come to see him. I wasn't prepared for what he was about to say. He told me that they were eliminating administrative assistant positions from the division. That statement was ridiculous. How could any division as busy as the sales department thrive successfully without administrative assistants? There was an entire national and international team of approximately fourteen people who depended on me daily for sales support. That was not going to change. Phones still needed to be answered, and letters need to be typed and sent out to clients. Products and contracts needed to be sent out to customers. The account managers were not going to do all that work themselves.

Unfortunately, this vice president let his ego get in the way at the expense of everyone else on his team. He just wanted to get rid of the person who dared to stand up to him. As the old saying goes, I wouldn't bow down or kiss up to him. The sales team was infuriated with his decision, but they feared him, so nobody challenged that decision. Later they took me out to lunch and gave me flowers because they felt so bad. Two of them provided exceptional references for me.

Jack couldn't say, "I don't have a legal reason to fire you, but I don't like you." Instead they eliminated my position on paper with a plan I am sure to resurrect it later and call it something else. That would keep them from getting into any legal hot water.

Anyway, I made sure I was not being fired and that it was my job that was being eliminated. He had the nerve to tell me I could stay and finish up things, but my last day would be on a certain date two weeks away. Do you know I actually contemplated going back and finishing the work on my desk? There was a lot on my desk. In fact, I was right in the middle of a major international project. At first, the loyalty virtue within kicked in for a minute. Then I went home and talked with my older brother, Thaddeus, who brought me back to my senses. He said, "You better not go back to work!"

One of the deacons at my church, who was a schoolteacher, told me that two weeks' severance was not enough for my years of service.

When I told my brother I refused to cry, he said, "You better cry and cry a lot." By the time I called Human Resources on the next day, the tears were flowing. According to her, two weeks' severance pay was reasonable. For that reason, I started crying more and told her about all the injustices I had suffered at the hand of Jack. I said, "You don't know what I've been through."

Consequently, when she called me the next day, the severance package had increased from two weeks to two months. No doubt, I had put the fear of God in them.

With family and friends as my support, I challenged the decision regarding my severance package. My sister-in-law and I met with the HR person at InfoData. My sister-in-law was dressed in a suit, so the HR person didn't know if she was my lawyer. We didn't identify who she was. At this meeting, I informed her I was not signing the severance agreement and gave her a page-and-a-half letter addressed to the president of InfoData, Tom. The HR person and the legal general counsel were copied. In this letter, I outlined the injustices that had been going on in the sales division since Jack joined the company.

Let me pause here and say to executives who like to play games, don't underestimate the power of your assistant. She or he is privy to everything that goes on and knows things you don't think she or he knows. They are listening and looking when you think they are not. You can find yourself in a legal battle because you were not smart enough to dot every *i* and cross every *t*. In fact, we have a PhD in a course called "the stupid things bosses say and do."

On the day I came to meet with the HR person, I saw Jack walk through the doors. He had a smirk on his face. I heard later that he didn't have a smirk on his face when he was called into a meeting with the HR person and the general counsel. In fact, he became angry when he heard what my accusations were. Sorry, partner, you were not going to have the last say. Do you think I would just be invisible and slip away into the corporate sunset? At that point, the invisible woman was very visible. This invisible woman had now become a visible woman that InfoData had to negotiate an agreement with.

Soon after that meeting, the president's assistant called me to set up an appointment to discuss my letter. Before I met with the president of the company, I went to a prominent law firm in the city to see if they would take my case. The senior attorney charged $200 an hour, and his assistant would charge $150. Both were above my budget, especially since I hadn't signed their agreement to get my severance. Fortunately, the younger lawyer said I could negotiate my own case. The senior lawyer did say I could get up to six months' severance.

When I met with Tom, he tried to assume responsibility for the way Jack had treated me, but I wouldn't let him. The bottom line is this: Jack didn't like me. That's too bad. I didn't like him either. I told Tom that the lawyer said I was entitled to six months' severance. His whole face changed, and he said, "I am not giving you six months' vacation." Instead, we agreed that they would pay me up to six months' severance as long as I was actively looking for a job. The HR person checked in with me regularly to see what I was doing.

Clearly, Tom thought I had a good case against Jack. Having six months to look for a job meant I didn't have to be desperate and accept any position. Additionally, a friend of mine was already looking for a job for me.

Included in that package were psychologist's visits and an employment counseling service. After meeting with the psychologist one time, he said, "There is nothing wrong with you." He also confirmed that companies could legally fire you because they don't like you. Yet the president of the company somehow felt I could cause trouble. That's why he approved the plan of paying me six months' severance while I looked for a job. What a great feeling that was. I was visible! Do you see me now, Jack?

The employment counseling service gave me good advice for obtaining a new job. One of the main thing she said was "Don't talk about Jack." Then they retyped my résumé and produced an excellent professional tool.

After that, I called the law firm to get my files and told the younger lawyer what was agreed. She congratulated me and said, "We need to hire you." I didn't tell her, but I know this is what we call the favor of God. Throughout my employment history, God has given me wisdom, confidence, and strength to fight and win battles. They had no idea the firepower I had backing me up.

It took three months to find the job that best fit me. That was the best job search I ever had. I wasn't nervous or stressed because I knew I didn't have to accept anything. A paycheck was steadily coming in, and I knew I was in control of the process. I enjoyed having all the major holidays off, and I took the advice of my career counselor, who said, "Don't wait until the severance time is over, but look for a job now."

During the job search, I interviewed at a company for an executive assistant position that would be the assistant to the president of the company. As the interviewer walked into the room, I could tell by the look on her face that I was not the right color for the job. The interview was over in about thirty minutes, but not before I had some fun and played with her. After she finished asking her questions, I asked her, "Are you sure there are no more questions you want to ask me?" She said, "No, I can see you are very qualified."

In reality, I wanted to say, "Don't worry, I don't want to be an assistant to the president of your company. At this stage in my life, I don't feel like doing personal things for anyone." No doubt I was having flashbacks about a woman we will call Helen, who was the executive assistant to the president of a company I used to work for. Helen was one of the sweetest persons you will ever meet. I can still see her smile. There were lines on her face that indicated her journey had not been easy. Although she was the most powerful executive assistant in the company, she was a very humble person with a difficult job. She had to have a pad of paper by her phone at home at all times so the president could call her at any time and give her instructions. When I first got transferred to the main office of Water Storage Company, I also assisted Helen. One time I transcribed a tape the president had dictated to her. There was nothing on that tape that related to company business. Instead it was about securing his boat for the winter and ordering a special type of sole for his shoes. That experience made me laugh because I didn't have to deal with him on a permanent basis, and definitely didn't have to interact with him at home. Thankfully that was a temporary position.

When I accepted my new position at the Starlight Company, the president of InfoData, Tom, sent me flowers and congratulated me. He wrote on the card, "I knew you could find another job." I laughed when I read his note. He probably wanted to say, "I am glad you are finally off my payroll."

In time, the sales at InfoData dropped considerably, and Jack was no longer the star vice president of sales. He was fired. Sometime later that company went out of business due to some mismanagement of the company funds. Jack did me a favor by eliminating my job, but I had great satisfaction emerging out of there as a visible woman. Unfortunately, when I retired years later, I could not collect any pension from that defunct company.

Starlight Company

The invisible syndrome can be experienced from your peers. When I joined the Starlight Company (SC), I joined a division that was in a developmental stage. They were a part of a new product line that had not launched or went live. My director, Sally, was new, and our positions were also in the developmental stages. We were both trying to figure out how our positions would evolve. It became obvious quickly that she could not provide enough work to keep me busy. Therefore, I gladly took on supporting the case manager director and her staff. The reputation of my excellence, good nature, and willingness to help spread throughout the department. The staff I supported was happy.

That joy was not experienced by everyone in the department. In fact, it ignited jealousy within one of the administrative secretaries. Without consulting with my bosses or me, she and the other administrative secretary wrote a memo stating that if anyone needed help, they should contact one of them. My name wasn't mentioned. It was like I didn't exist—I was invisible again. One of the administrative secretaries was supposed to be my Christian friend. With hurt feelings, I approached my friend about the memo, and she acted clueless, as though she didn't understand my concerns. When I showed my direct supervisor, Sally, the memo, she responded, "What are you, chopped liver? Don't worry. I am being transferred to the Boston office, and my boss said I could bring you along with me. Besides, they have a better cafeteria there." The invisible syndrome was being removed again. My director could have left me there, but her choice to bring me with her meant I was valuable. The other director was saddened by my departure.

Being transferred to Boston felt like history repeating itself. Again, I was being transferred from a smaller office to the corporate headquarters. I was glad to be able to use public transportation again. Sadly, I was transferred to Boston just in time to witness the massive layoffs that was happening at SC. Because I was the new kid on the block, I knew the morning that Maria called me into her office, I was on my way out the door. Instead, I was told about the layoffs, and I was now her new assistant. The other person with more seniority was let go. I enjoyed working with her and was sad when she left. Maria was my boss when my two brothers, Thaddeus and Sherwin, died five months apart. Having her as a boss helped me to navigate through this very sad time in my life. She not only valued me but she gave me little gifts along the way to say thank you.

Shortly after her departure, a promotion opportunity occurred. That promotion would require me to work for a gentleman we will call David. Quickly I discovered that a promotion was not necessarily a good thing. The staff who worked for David was somewhat intimidated by him. He had them jumping and scrambling when he wanted things done. His personality could go from being calm to explosive in a matter of seconds. When he got in those irritating moods and snapped at me, I just looked at him as though he had two heads. I felt like saying I am not intimidated by you. This is not my first rodeo, and I had been in this business too long and had survived dealing with executives like you.

In spite of his emotional outbursts, our relationship started out great. I felt valuable, but then the invisible syndrome reoccurred again. A man we will call Ron was his right-hand man. He started saying negative things about me. Ron and I had a disagreement regarding the seriousness of a mistake I had made. He kept bringing it up as though it was a life-changing event. Eventually I got irritated and let him know that I thought he was making a big deal out of nothing. From that time on, he set out to poison David's mind about me. In fact, he worked on a plan to get me out of that position. His ego was fragile, and he didn't like the idea that I disagreed with him. One morning I came in earlier than they anticipated. Ron and David were having a conversation. By the guilty looks on their faces, I knew they were talking about me. After that morning, David started hovering over me to see what I was doing and even questioned me about office supplies I ordered. Why would a senior leader of a company care about what supplies I ordered? He no longer trusted me. My workstation was at the end of the hall where an aisle was located. One day David came quietly around that corner as though he thought he would catch me doing something wrong. That was crazy!

Ron succeeded in convincing David that I shouldn't be in that position. One of the other executive assistant's boss was leaving the company. They decided they would give her my position. I said then and I will say it again: If they wanted to give her that position, they could have just given it to her. They did not have to try and humiliate and destroy my reputation in the process. At that point, I was tired of working with David. I was tied to that desk, and I really missed the freedom of being able to move around more.

Before my performance evaluation, Ron tried to get me to say some negative things about David, but I knew that was a setup. Why, Judas, would I trust you? Then he tried to get me to work for him. Why would I want to work for you? You don't think I am smart enough to figure out that you started this negative energy between David and me? That was not my first corporate position. I had already been adequately educated by leaders smarter than you. If I was so incompetent, why would you want me to work for you? When I refused to play his little corporate game, he wrote up a negative performance evaluation about me. David signed the review and presented it to me, but the handwriting on the evaluation was Ron's.

I have that evaluation in hand at this writing. Out of the nine categories, six were 4s, meaning "needs improvement." Yet the overall rating was 3, meaning "meets expectations."

The performance evaluation was a sham. They evaluated me on stuff that wasn't part of my job description. Please, people, read my résumé. I worked in HR and managed the evaluation process. I am not a novice. Rather, I am a veteran of corporate war. Yet that is the tool they used to justify my demotion and reason I would no longer be working for David.

Although I had been in the corporate arena for a while, I did not expect this chapter to end like this. That was a painful day in my life, which left me shocked and hurt. They caught me off guard, ambushed if you will. Unfortunately, I was unable to gather my thoughts or keep my emotions together. Literally I had a meltdown when Ron took me into a different room to meet with my new boss, and my tears flowed uncontrollably. The invisible syndrome was crossing my path again. Ron gave me two options: (1) I could work for a manager in this same division, whom we will call Rosy, or (2) find a position in another department. Rosy interrupted him and said, "Gwen, you and I always got along." Ron had the nerve to say that Betty was the solution and she would now work for David. That sentiment didn't last long. She was human like me, made mistakes, and disagreed with him. When the honeymoon was over, I was so tempted to ask him, "Is Betty still your solution?"

Other people I knew, including my previous director, Sally, told me that this wasn't my fault. David had a reputation of not being nice. She even advised me to submit a complaint to HR. Before I could make that decision, my maternal grandmother died, and it took all the energy I had to cope with the grieving process. A friend helped me to pack my stuff and to move through the back halls so that I could be spared more embarrassment.

Before I found out my grandmother died, I had decided to take some time off to regroup. During that time, I bought a new computer and christened it by writing a memo to David and Ron. That memo contradicted all the lies they wrote and let them know they were both liars. Although I copied HR, I never delivered that memo to them, but wanted them to think I did. Upon my return, I promptly delivered that memo to David and Ron.

Following are some excerpts from the memo I wrote to them.

> I have read my Performance Feedback more carefully, and reflected on my over 25 years of experience within the corporate arena. One of the things I have come to understand is that performance reviews are a matter of perception. Depending on who is writing the performance evaluation, it can vary from person to person. Yet, I must admit, I have never received a negative performance evaluation in over 25 years until now. I have always prided myself in excelling in whatever position I have been in.
>
> Then it became clear to me, that in this case, the perception has been tainted. A plan was put in place to put someone else in my position. That someone, no doubt, you felt would have a better rapport with. Therefore, a negative performance was written about me in an attempt to discredit my performance and justify your decision.
>
> As I stated verbally, I do not agree with this evaluation, and I have written a response to each "4" rating I received.

Below is an abbreviated evaluation of what they wrote and how I responded.

1. Personal Mastery / Technical Expertise

Ron wrote: "Demonstrated some difficulty handling multiple assignments simultaneously without coaching/direction."

My response: "I have no recollection of having difficulty in handling multiple assignments simultaneously. As far as receiving coaching/directions, I received neither. I had to learn things by trial and error in this position. There were no guidelines in place. For the record, I previously supported a fourteen-person international sales force and successfully handled multiple assignments simultaneously. So handling multiple assignments has never been a problem."

2. Leadership

Ron wrote: "Has not shown any understanding of her role to assist David in organizing and directing division activities."

My response: "When I started this position, it became clear to me rather quickly that there was already an inner circle of managerial staff in place that David relied on for assistance in organizing and directing the division's activities. There was no room for my advice, assistance, or opinion."

3. Initiative

Ron wrote: "Did not consistently identify activities or issues to advance without being prompted by others."

My response: "This statement is unclear, and I have no idea what you are referring to, so I won't even give a response."

4. Communication

Ron wrote: "Inconsistent in providing regular updates to David (e.g., schedule) and in checking for details on messages and schedules."

My response: "David has several people who add or subtract from his schedule, including him. There have been times when I have not been notified myself about changes. The assumption is being made that I was always kept informed and did not keep him informed, and that is not the case. As far as taking messages, I am very detailed when I record messages. As far as the verbal statement about voice messaging, I always ask if I can take a message in order to find out if I can help them. There were people who were adamant about being transferred into the voice message system, especially since some were of personal nature."

5.   Adaptability/Flexibility

Ron wrote: "Clearly showed willingness to follow through on changes, etc. Yet appeared sometimes unable to act quickly in most dynamic circumstances."

My response: "Again, I have no recollection of such an occasion. I have always acted quickly in all circumstances."

6.   Business Understanding

Ron wrote: "Has shown a basic understanding of business, but has not achieved a level that is required for issues addressed by division."

My response: "Again, I don't know what the phrase is referring to. A required level of business understanding for the Division was not communicated to me, so how can I even be rated on such an unclear standard?"

> In summary, I have done an excellent job in this Division for the last 10 months, and should have been rated higher. Let it go on record, that I should have received a "3" or "2" in all categories.
>
> Note: I have not signed the Performance Feedback form, because I feel my signature will convey that I agree with it when I don't.

I gave them both a package with my response after I returned from my bereavement leave.

For the record, that job was not challenging. Most days I had to work hard at finding something to do. It was more of a babysitting job than anything else. Clearly, Ron must have been drinking when he wrote this evaluation, because it did not make any practical sense. They certainly did not expect me to challenge him.

Someone said that success is the best revenge. Working with Rosy turned out to be one of the best career moves in my life. I will always be grateful for Rosy's friendship and mentoring. She not only took me under her wings and mentored me but she wrote raving reviews about me that said I was not the incompetent person they said I was.

Further, what is so funny is that they had to approve percentages and bonuses I received. They never blocked any. In fact, they smiled and spoke to me as though nothing wrong had happened.

Doubtless, they probably were glad I didn't pursue going to HR. When you go to HR, you need to have a well-thought-out plan, because they have not been trained to help us. Sorry, my experience has been that they are always on management's side. They may seem sympathetic at first, but they always come back and try to get you to conform to management's expectations. There wasn't a plan in place, so I had to try and get along with them. Besides, I really enjoyed the work I was doing.

The position I came into allowed me the space and freedom to grow beyond the administrative role. Rosy changed my title without having to ask her and moved me up to the next level. This position not only gained me respect as a professional but it brought me into the spotlight. Although people didn't know the face behind the name, they knew my name. I would meet people at different events that I had organized, and they would say, "Oh, you are Gwen Wheeler." Yes, the invisible woman had now become visible again.

I wish I could tell you that my career at Starlight Corporation ended on this successful chapter, but it didn't. As I said earlier, "Change is inevitable. Change is constant." Someone else said, "Change is inevitable. Growth is optional." We should all desire to grow through every season of our life.

Other challenges within this company are blended within the pages of other chapters. When possible, I will point it out.

CHAPTER 2

· · · ◆ ◆ ● ◆ ◆ · ·

The Corporate Halls of Pain and Change Can Be Devastating!

The invisible syndrome can be caused by pain and unexpected change. Because these two elements often overlap, I have brought them together in one chapter. People's perception determines how bosses evaluate and interact with you. Although you are the same person, two bosses can see you differently. One boss may greatly value you and gives you the expectation that you will ascend successfully the corporate ladder. While another boss may find you a threat or the chemistry doesn't mesh.

Unfortunately, if the boss who finds you a threat is your present boss, your once-promising career can abruptly come to an end. Before the end occurs, you may have to endure daily battles with a hostile, immature person, who tries to make you feel invisible. That person may constantly look for ways to degrade you, hoping you will quit. If that plan doesn't work, his next step may be to find a legal way to fire you. Oftentimes firing a person who has been an outstanding employee may be a difficult task because others know that person is not incompetent. Sadly, corporations will not stand up to that corporate bully. Instead, they came up with a strategy they call restructuring. They will reconstruct your department and reconstruct you out of a job.

Understandably, that hurts, and your reaction may be "How can this person do this to me?" You feel invisible. Yet somebody gave them the power to force you to leave without a justifiable reason. Sadly, legally they can do that unless you signed a contract with them at the beginning of your employment. It's called employment at will. Employment at will means that an employee can be terminated at any time without any reason, explanation, or warning.

In chapter 1, I stated a principle my professor taught us in Systems Theory of Psychology. He said, "There should always be a learning process in everything we do." What should we learn from a company's policy of employee at will? Keep your résumé uploaded and updated continuously. If you experience employment termination, find a healthy way to regroup from that negative experience. What are some practical ways to regroup from employment termination? First, take a deep breath, stop, and pause. Then say these words, "My life is not over! That experience will not destroy me. This is a new beginning, an opportunity to evolve into a better me." Along with this positive self-talk, it may be necessary to sit down with a professional employment counselor, who can help you recover from the emotional and psychological trauma of losing a job. That same person may be able to help you take practical steps to explore job opportunities. If you were at your last job for a long period of time, you definitely need to talk to someone about the present job market. The interviewing process changes continuously. In addition, you may need to take some classes and think about changing your career goals. Just be open to new possibilities.

Generally, when employment termination occurs, many people are too far from retirement and not ready to make the transition into self-employment. Self-employment has its own set of challenges. Therefore, plan your strategy for moving forward: find another job.

Equally important is your own self-support. Encourage yourself because others don't know you like you know yourself. Appreciate and become aware of the person you have become. Celebrate your gifts and talents. Create your own bonus system to reward yourself for a job well done. Place motivational signs around your home like these: "The greatest pleasure in life is doing what people say you cannot do." "Sparkle." "Stop dreaming and start doing." "Think big. Dream big" "Do something great today!" "Dream the impossible!"

Another Change at Starlight

As you keep those motivational ideas in view, remember what I wrote earlier. "Change is inevitable. Change is constant." Change is a lifetime of experiences. Although I became visible at Starlight, change came again. The invisible syndrome abruptly showed up in my life.

After moving forward in my next position at the Starlight Corporation, it felt good that things were going well. This was a safe haven for a while, but then change occurred again. Rosy made the decision to leave her position and pursue something else. The new director, which we will call Drake, was young, self-centered, and arrogant. He wasn't always diplomatic and could be quite insensitive. After we met to discuss my job responsibilities, he responded, "That's not rocket science." That statement started the invisible syndrome flowing again and made me feel that he didn't think what I did was any big deal. When I reminded him later about that statement, he didn't remember saying that. He assured me that he thought what I did was very valuable.

Then the unexpected happened in the second month of working for this new director. My mother had her first stroke while I was away at a conference. Understandably, my life was thrown into a chaotic web of sadness and distress. Thankfully, she survived the stroke, but the road to recovery was long, stressful, and painful. My mother was the center of my world, so for a while I was in a state of grief. The mother I knew, loved, and relied heavily upon was changed physically, mentally, and emotionally. The strong, independent mother I had known all my life was now depending on me. Dementia began to creep in slowly.

A cloud of gloom and weariness hang over my head daily and showed on my face. From the beginning of this painful event, Drake showed no compassion or sympathy. In fact, he completely forgot about the fact that my mother had had a stroke. He interpreted my sad countenance to mean I no longer wanted to work for him. One day he called me into his office and yelled at me. Yes, yelled at me and said, "If you don't want to work for me anymore, I can arrange for you to work for someone else." Confused at first but then to the best of my ability I tried to explain that I was having a difficult time coping with my mother having a stroke. His response was "You are bringing me down. Other people are having problems with their mother, and you are supposed to be a Christian." I wanted to say, "Really, buddy? You are supposed to be a Christian too, but I don't see the love of Jesus flowing out of you today." He missed the part about compassion during his new member's class.

Clearly, we needed a break from each other, so we agreed I would take a couple of days off to regroup. Did those couple of days off help me? No, but I did what a lot of folks do in corporate America: I put a smiley mask on. I changed the color of my hair and put on makeup to cover up the pain. When I would get to the elevator before going upstairs, I would tell myself to put on the mask because nobody wanted to deal with my pain.

When I returned to work and was able to mask the pain, he asked what had happened. Really? At first he tried to make me feel that something was wrong with me because I was sad that the woman who birthed me was in the hospital recovering from a stroke. Then he wanted me to tell him how I was now coping. How about this answer: none of your business! Actually, I don't remember what I said to him, but I am sure it wasn't anything deep. Yet there were days I couldn't mask the pain and would tell him I was having a bad day so I wouldn't get yelled at. Tears sometimes cannot be controlled.

Mom's recovery had a lot of twists and turns to walk through. At one point she had recovered enough to come home and be at home by herself, but she had a hearing problem. Therefore, I had to speak loudly so she could hear me. Drake called me into his office and reprimanded me for talking so loud and being emotional. At first I asked my mother not to call me at work, and then I snapped out of that insanity and realized that my eighty-year-old mother had the right to call me at my job.

The next time he called me into his office and yelled at me, I wasn't so nice. I yelled back at him and said, "You don't know what I am going through. I fight every day to keep my head above water! Besides, other people in this area talk loud too, but I am the only one you have a problem with." By the look on his face, I think I made him nervous. You wonder why employees have breakdowns on the job and become either suicidal or homicidal? It is because of insensitive bosses like Drake.

In my opinion, most directors and managers haven't been properly trained on how to deal with employees who are going through major life crisis, especially the younger ones. Their parents can still go dancing and play with their grandchildren. After that emotional conversation, he wrote me an email and asked how he could help. We agreed that I could work from home one day a week. He offered the use of his office when I had to have one of those intense conversations with my mother. One of my coworkers was laughing about me talking loudly, so I walked over to him and said, "This isn't funny!" Then I gave him an earful of what I was dealing with, and the smile came off his face.

Since I was my mother's primary caregiver, I took her to most of her doctor's appointments. Drake said to me one day, "Your family isn't being fair to the Starlight Corporation." As my sister, Pat, would say, "Oh really?" I could have said, "You are not being fair to me when you don't hire a backup, and I have to take my laptop home during vacations and holidays to oversee the company events I manage."

Again, his lack of compassion was due to his age. Both of his parents were younger than mine and healthy. He couldn't relate to my generation who find themselves in a season of having to take care of an ailing parent or parents. There was a baby monitor between my mother's room and mine. A good night's sleep was a thing of the past, and I worried about her all the time. I was stressed every day. If I called home and my mother didn't pick up the phone or the line was busy, I went into a panic. My niece Jasmine would go by and check on her.

A Change that Broke My Heart

The tension between Drake and I ebbed, but then the head of our division retired, and Drake reported to Ron. Our division was reconstructed behind closed doors. New reporting relations were revealed at a special division meeting. One of my worst nightmares was discovered by looking at an organization chart. When you think you can't be kicked down any lower, then it happens. The organization chart showed I would now report to Greg, who should never have been promoted to this new position in the first place. He was a horrible person to work with, worse than Drake, and I did not like him at all. Further, my feelings were hurt because I felt Drake could have given me the common courtesy to tell me privately that I would no longer be working for him. The invisible syndrome returned. In my opinion, giving people organization charts to inform them their life was changing was impersonal and unprofessional. They might as well scream out, "We don't think you are valuable. You are invisible to us!" When would this invisible syndrome stop showing up?

After the general meeting, we then divided into smaller groups, and Drake asked me what I thought about the change. I was so angry that I could hardly look at him, but my response was priceless. My words were, "You really don't want to know." He was shocked at my response. My heart was beating so fast that I felt like I was having a heart attack. Of all mornings, I forgot to take my blood pressure medication. I went to the cafeteria to check my pressure, and of course it was high. At that point I knew I needed to go home, so I went back upstairs to get my laptop just in time to run in Drake. Now he wanted to talk. My response was "My blood pressure is high, and I am going home." When I got outside to wait for the train, I fell against the fence and started crying uncontrollably. It felt like my world was crumbling. The words I said to my coworker echoed in my mind, "I will not work for Greg!" Quitting without a plan was not an option. Corporate America won't pay you if you just quit. A plan had to be developed. Another form of income had to be found.

When I got home and had time to clear my head, I wrote the following email to Drake.

> I want to clear the air and summarize my feelings about yesterday's division meeting/announcements. I have been in corporate life for approximately 36 years, and have worked closely with the senior management of companies. I felt yesterday's announcements were handled in a very impersonal manner. It was like we were all strangers brought into a big room to be told about relationships, yes, relationships changes. I don't know what consultant told you all that it was OK to do it that way, but it really wasn't. I felt private meetings should have been held first.
>
> Today I am at peace with this and grateful that this isn't my whole world/life. It doesn't define who I am. I am confident that as my church teaches, "something good will come out of this," and I will become better because of it. *("I would have lost heart, unless I had believed that I would see the goodness of the Lord in the land of the living"* [Psalms 27:13].)

Drake wrote me back as follows:

> Thanks for the email! I had zero to do with the way things were handled. I will pass on your sentiment to Ron and the CEO. I can assure you that no consultant told us to do it that way. I personally tried to have 1:1 meetings after the fact, but few people took me up on my offer other than Mack. You decided you didn't want to talk yesterday." [My editorial: He missed the whole point. People wanted a discussion before the meeting, not afterward.]

I am still puzzled [because we haven't had a chance to discuss] why you appear to be upset at this change? Is it because you will not be reporting directly to me? Is it because you have a problem with Greg? Your role is not changing—same responsibilities, same salary, internal communications.

I am more than happy to sit down and discuss in person rather than trading emails. This new arrangement will definitely be a change for all of us. Have a good weekend!

My response to his email:

Thanks for the response and some clarification, but as I said earlier I am a peace with this. I am moving forward with optimism and no further discussion is necessary. As the old cliché goes, it has become "Water under the bridge." Enjoy the weekend; I plan to enjoy mine and recover from this head cold and sore throat. I hear it is supposed to be cold tomorrow. P.S. Congratulations on your promotion to vice president; I wish you well in your new role.

Note: I purposely didn't address the issue about working with Greg, and wasn't going to put that in writing anyway. All the niceties I wrote were just to throw Drake off track until I came up with a strategy to get another job. My years of being in corporate America taught me a lot of things, and I was not going to give this man any rope to hang me. This is called strategy—don't tell the enemy your secrets.

After a few days, I calmed down further and returned to work. Temporarily I decided I would work for Greg, but not as his assistant. When I told Drake I wasn't going to be Greg's assistant because I was evolving out of that role before he came, he said, "Greg needed support too." I restrained myself from saying, "You are telling me this because you think I care. You just treated me like I was invisible." He was then trying to have a conversation about the change they made. It was too late at that point. Damage was done. He was so busy enjoying being promoted to vice president that he never thought how these changes would affect the rest of us. He was one of the few in that division who got something good out of the change. Greg was one of them.

Greg, from the very start, was rude. I would walk into his office to ask him a question, and he would say, "What?" I walked out immediately so I wouldn't punch him in the face.

Could somebody please explain to me why when there are major changes in the structure of companies they find the most obnoxious people to fill pivotal roles? You want the change to go smoothly, but you put a self-absorbed person in a role he is not qualified to be in. Because a person graduated from college doesn't mean he is a good manager. He has no people skills and is not diplomatic or caring.

Whenever one of my coworkers met with Greg, he said it was like being on a blind date. It was awkward. This person was rude in meetings. If you, even his boss, disagreed with him, he had temper tantrums. In an effort to cooperate, I took on more responsibility and was still allowed to work from home one day a week with flexible hours. Through a communication vehicle, I discovered Greg was sending negative emails to Drake about me. I didn't say anything because I still didn't have a plan. He thought when we were in the midst of a snowstorm that this fifty-plus-old woman should ask a thirty-five-year-old man if she could stay home. Little boy, that wasn't the way things worked. I wrote and said I wasn't coming in. He wrote Drake and said he was going to speak to me. Drake must have told him not to say anything, which was a good thing. Without doubt I would have given him an education he wouldn't have forgotten about for a while.

As my mother's health continued to deteriorate, we decided to put her in a senior citizen daycare program, which required us to turn all her life insurance policies over to a funeral home. We decided to go ahead and make prearrangements for her funeral as well. That was hard. We scheduled it on a day that I worked from home. Since I was quitting early, I let Greg know what I was doing. It was only thirty minutes earlier. Why did I do that? Trying to keep honest.

Here's my email:

> Good morning, I am logging in a little earlier than normal because I have a 2:00 appointment with a funeral home to do some more pre-planning for my mother. I will try and check my email when I return. But I am not feeling great today, so I might just sign off when I go for my appointment.

He wrote this email to me:

> Thanks for the heads-up. I'm sorry you not feeling well. [No mention about my mom's preplanning.]
>
> By the way, have you been tracking your hours to make sure you're fulfilling the regular hour work week and coming in at the designated time. I have not been paying attn. to it as I trust that you'll take care of it. Drake mentioned as we discussed that you were going to come in every day at designated time.
>
> Anyway, I apologize I've been so busy and have not rescheduled our check-in meeting."

From the surface, it doesn't seem like he wrote anything wrong, but it rubbed me the wrong way. I felt he was insinuating that I wasn't giving Starlight the hours they required of me. Was this how I was being rewarded for being honest about thirty minutes? The main issue here was he was questioning me on the wrong day about my time. I was preplanning my mom's funeral. In hindsight, I am sure I overreacted. If my mother wasn't sick, my emotions and mind would have been calmer.

I responded to his email and I copied Drake. Here is what I wrote:

> Hi Greg,
>
> Drake and I discussed this again at my review (my time). I am sure you all know that my life is not normal right now. I am living through one of the worst times in my life. But we also discussed months ago that if I didn't make it in by designated time I would make up the time and I do. There are nights I work later, and when I am feeling well I put in extra time when I am working from home.
> My mother's condition has worsened, and I am doing the best I can right now. I can't promise that I will be at work daily at designated time, but I will make up my time.

Greg didn't like the idea that I put this in writing and copied Drake. He said it was not the best way, but I said I wanted it in writing. He said, "Oh." I wanted Drake to see that I was being harassed about my time.

Further, I was the one that took my laptop home during holidays, vacations, and snowstorms to stay on top of things because I did not have a backup. I managed the major corporate events. It was insulting for him to question me about my time. In addition, I had five weeks of vacation plus sick time.

My emotions exploded. All I could envision are the nights I worked late and the days I did trudge through the snow to complete events. One night, one of the attorneys saw me working late and said, "Do you know there is a major snowstorm out there?" What I needed from my present boss, Greg, was the acknowledgment that I was in a painful time in my life. Preplanning for a parent's funeral is indescribably painful. Again, he was young and naturally insensitive.

In any event, all this made me realize it was time to leave the Starlight Corporation. I was too old and had put too much time in to have to put up with that nonsense. The idiotic comments from his boss, Drake, in the past were tolerated, but I was not going to put up with his ignorance.

The strategy to leave Starlight was not a clear, well-thought-out plan. My lawyer actually said, "You are a nice person, but you wrote too much." He actually convinced me later that I would not win this case. I was almost convinced that this was a losing battle, but the Almighty God I serve told me to persevere.

In anticipation of leaving, I took my personal things home little by little. A security guard saw me coming out with my box and no doubt thought I had been laid off.

The lawyer was right. The writer in me wrote too many facts that were actually held against me at first. They were trying to convince me that I had resigned, but I corrected that in writing. I tried to reach a favorable settlement with HR, but they were playing games at the instructions of Ron. Yes, he was at it again, trying to push the knife deeper into my back. At first, the HR rep tried to pretend she was concerned and would help me, but the real colors came through. They tried to come up with one last scheme to get me to come back to work on their terms.

With this in mind, they set up a meeting to demand that I still work for Greg. We were in a major companywide project that they wanted me to finish. A young HR rep we will call Nancy met with me to tell me about this wonderful plan and how she would monitor me. You are kidding me, right? That day I was having stroke-like symptoms, and I wasn't going back to work before seeing my doctor. This young girl thought she would make me go upstairs by telling me, "You owe the company deliverables." She threatened me and said, "If you don't go back to work today, that would be considered your resignation." I told her, "You don't have that in writing." Then she went from the threat of resignation to termination and told me her boss would be in touch with me. Understandably, I was upset. Then she started ranting, "You are not respecting me. This is insubordination. Your behavior is inappropriate. This would be considered a performance issue." All this was said because I was upset.

At this point, my inner alarm system started alerting me to get out of there. Suddenly, without a warning or any more words, I got up and left the meeting. The atmosphere was becoming very uncomfortable. Visions of the security guards walking in the room flooded my mind, and this prompted me to leave the room. She ran after me. Not wanting to alarm the security guard, I smiled at him so he wouldn't think anything was wrong. Again, I was experiencing hostility from the Starlight Corporation. I don't know what she told others happened at that meeting, but they then tried to use that meeting as the basis for my termination.

That evening I received two voice messages from Drake stating, "Gwen, this is Drake. I heard what happened at your meeting with HR. Please call me before you return to work. This is about your employment."

Consequently, I responded that night with my voice message, "Drake, this is Gwen, and I got both of your voice messages. For the record, I am not a well woman and have not been well for a while, but have managed somehow to work anyway. A few months ago I tried to convey the fact to you that being a caretaker for an ill mother was wearing on me and affecting my emotional well-being. Therefore, I was surprised that you willingly placed me in a working relationship with Greg. You knew it was destined for failure. Working with him has caused a great amount of unnecessary stress that has made me become more ill.

"I walked out of the meeting with Nancy because I found her unprofessional, immature, and unprepared for the task she was assigned to do. I tried to explain to her that I was ill, experiencing stroke-like symptoms, and needed to see my doctor, who could not see me until Monday. I have a history of stroke in my family. She then began to issue threats at me. First, she said this would be considered my resignation, which I knew wasn't true, and then threatened termination and other things. The atmosphere was becoming increasingly more uncomfortable, so I left. Anyway, I will call you on Monday after I come back from my doctor's appointment."

My doctor did issue a note to stay out for two weeks. I met with Nancy's boss shortly after that and Ron. He was looking strange while Nancy's boss, whom we will call Cindy, was making all these wonderful promises to me, and I believed her. She said, "You are going to like what we worked out for you." Then they shook hands with me.

Within a week, I received a letter from Cindy, and she wrote lie after lie. Written in that letter was stuff that didn't happen. She also wrote that I should apply for short-term disability, knowing full well I didn't qualify. Yet I was told if I didn't apply, I would be terminated by a certain date. What she didn't know was that the third-party vendor that handled short-term disability applications automatically put you on family leave so you won't lose your job.

The lawyer I met with said I didn't have a case and I should have never met with those two by myself. He said Ron was meant to be a witness, a false witness at that. In other words, they set me up.

Verbal injustice behind closed doors is hard to fight and prove. They can say whatever they want and tell others that you misunderstood what they meant.

Alas, I almost gave up on receiving justice from the Starlight Corporation, especially after the lawyer said I wouldn't win. Being a woman of prayer, I kept praying and believing. God was on my side, and it was prophesied that He would throw confusion into the enemy's camp. My church and family kept praying, and I felt I was supposed to write one more letter to formally tell them I didn't agree with what she wrote.

In the meantime, a representative from a third-party vendor called to see if I was returning to work on May 30. I said to her, "I don't know if I have a job." Her response was priceless. She said, "Yes, you do have a job, because we automatically put you on family leave so they couldn't fire you." Wow! Her call was the final ammunition I needed. I included that statement in the letter.

The Starlight Corporation didn't want me back, and I certainly didn't want to go back. As the cliché goes, they played themselves in an attempt to discredit me. Their evil plot failed, and they had to rule in my favor. The favor of God was with me all the way.

They gave me what I wanted monetarily and time-wise. I can't disclose what the settlement was because then you would put the rest of this puzzle together and figure out where I was working. It was an off-the-books deal.

What you need to know is this: they started out treating me like I was invisible and thought I was too stupid to know that somebody was lying to me. Again, read my résumé. My résumé outlines major companies I worked for with, top, senior leaders, including HR leaders. The plans you came up with were already used by others and typed up by me. I learned from the best.

So this invisible woman became visible again. They had to respect my requests and pay me accordingly.

Another Story from InfoData

Whenever new leadership is hired, inevitably there will be changes that will negatively affect others. Hence, a person is often faced with the question of how to successfully coincide with these changes. However, those plans should never include hurting someone else.

Unfortunately, Evelyn chose to betray someone who had faithfully and tireless worked with her for years. The person she chose to betray was me. My mentor and friend decided it was more important for her to fit into the boys' club than it was for her to support my cause. Jack had hired some players to be on his team, but Evelyn was inherited from the old regime. The boys' club was formed, and Evelyn was not invited to join. He catered to folks who stroked his fragile ego. One day I infuriated some of the guys when I told them they were a bunch of little Jacks running around. It was sickening. One of the guys pretended that he cared about me, but I later figured out he was the spy for Jack. That betrayal didn't hurt. Just another lesson learned. Evelyn found it difficult to stroke his ego because she had worked too hard to climb the corporate ladder and became the international sales manager on her own merits. That title lost its significance when Jack came.

Betraying me wasn't her plan at first because she was angry that she was demoted when Jack was hired as the new sales director. Eventually she realized this was the leadership in place, and there was nothing she could do about it. She decided to accept a well-known philosophy that says, "If you can't beat them, join them." That phrase meant that if someone is too strong for you to defeat, it is better to be on the same side as them.

Getting into the boys' club became her mission, but it was an unethical mission. She tried to use the betraying of me as her access into this club. The invisible syndrome was brewing behind closed doors, and I didn't know it. Through my own words and her observation, she knew there was a lot of tension between Jack and me. My vulnerability was created because I trusted a woman, who had been my mentor and friend. She trained me and once wrote exceptional reviews and gave me the highest percentage of raises for her staff. One year I received 12 percent, and everyone else got less. Because of her mission to betray me, she began giving off negative signals through the words she spoke to me. Her behavior caused me to make peace with Jack.

Please don't walk through the corporate halls with your eyes and ears closed. Betrayers give off signals, but don't let them know you know. Just adjust your actions and plans if necessary. Someone rightfully said, "Friendship is just another casualty on the way to power." You could not have convinced me that she would stab me so viciously in my back, but she did.

Being a child of God, I serve an Omniscient Father, who sees and hears all things. If you pray and listen to His voice, He will show you the plans the wicked has plotted against you. More than that, He will show you how to navigate through them and come out on top. Scripture says, "'For My thoughts are not your thoughts, Nor are your ways My ways,' says the Lord. 'For as the heavens are higher than the earth, So are My ways higher than your ways, And My thoughts than your thoughts.'" In layman's terms, sometimes He will tell you something that doesn't make sense to your human mind. The day and moment came when what I sensed God was telling me to do didn't make sense. "Go clean Jack's office." My response was "But, God, you see the way he has been treating me." Again, His instructions were clear, "Go clean Jack's office." Reluctantly I entered into his office that was nicknamed the black hole. As I was digging through the piles of papers so I could organize and file things away, I discovered something that shocked, hurt, and made me angry. Evelyn had made a copy of a previous performance evaluation that had raving reviews. She crossed out the positive comments and replaced them with negative ones and even called me a clock watcher.

On the contrary, I wasn't a clock watcher. That term originated because of an event change in my life. My schedule changed because I was taking college courses at night. In order to get to the classes on time, I had to leave work on time, not early. That happened two nights a week. By the way, that's another thing about corporate America that really makes me angry. Some think it is only okay for certain employees to improve themselves by returning to college. They frown upon others and try to make them feel like they are not doing their job, especially when they have to leave early or on time.

Incidentally, Evelyn conveniently forgot about the nights I stayed late and went to Federal Express and DHL offices located in another part of the city because our mail room was closed. Going beyond the normal expectations of my job was how clients received contracts and products in a timely matter. The majority of her clients were international. When she was out of the country, I worked with technical support to make sure every problem was resolved with her clients. Every fax was answered in a timely matter. We had a twenty-four-hour turnaround policy. My efforts helped her to make sales quotas, for which I didn't get a percentage of her bonus checks or recognition. Frankly, this was an assistant account manager's job responsibilities, and I did it even after I was denied a promotion or recognition. That's called loyalty. Clearly, I did not deserve this betrayal.

Nevertheless, when things like this happen, you have to take a deep breath. Don't respond emotionally or immediately. Devise a plan of response that works best for you and your career. Then execute your plan in a professional manner. She betrayed me, and it hurt a lot. Yet I could not allow that hurt to cripple or control me. Instead I had to put a plan in place so I could survive this personal attack.

With this in mind, I decided to put that performance evaluation in a folder marked "Pending File." It was placed on top in his in-box so it could be easily found. By the way, I decided not to say anything to either of them about it. Of course, he found it and told her about it. After she came out of his office one afternoon, she nervously came to my desk and asked me, "How are you?" I looked at her and said, "I am fine." Neither of us mentioned that performance evaluation. I am sure she didn't know how to handle the fact that her plot to discredit me was uncovered. That was just another lesson-learned experience. Thank you, Evelyn, for teaching me that you were no longer my friend, and I couldn't trust you.

Surprisingly, her plan failed. Jack discounted what she wrote about me and gave me a good review. He wanted to destroy this former close-boss/employee network, and she fell right into his plans. He had a smirk on his face the day he told her I knew. Regrettably, she destroyed a relationship with a person who was one of her strongest allies. Further, her betrayal did not win her a membership into the boys' club. Instead, she was respected less, alienated more, and did not advance her career. In fact, he promoted the male friend whom he hired. Let's call him Grant. Grant liked and appreciated me.

For these reasons, Evelyn became angry and hostile and publicly made negative remarks about Jack. Obviously she felt that injustice had occurred since she had been there longer. Her hard work was not recognized, and she experienced the invisible syndrome. Welcome to my world!

One More Story about Paul

During my earlier years in corporate America, you never thought about standing up to your bosses and letting them know when you felt you were unjustly treated. You let them make you feel invisible. That was until I had enough with a few of my bosses. One day Paul had yelled at me for something that wasn't my fault. My first reaction was to cry later after he walked away. Friends tried to comfort me. Then I went home that night, regrouped, and requested to meet with him the next day. In a very professional manner, I said to him, "I am human, and when I make a mistake, I don't want to be yelled at. My bosses are not perfect, and they shouldn't expect me to be." He tried to act as though he didn't know what I was talking about, but I quickly informed him about his actions the previous day. I should have ended the conversation by saying, "Is that assertive enough for you?"

Generally speaking, many of us experience new bosses who don't like us, small increases in pay, and unfair evaluations. When you get what you consider to be an unfair evaluation, be bold and write within your evaluation what you have done. If there is no room in your written review, create an addendum. Don't let your manager have the final say. Choose not to allow them to make you feel invisible/invaluable. Please don't sign the evaluation if you don't agree with it.

Furthermore, please have an advancement goal in mind and write it down with practical steps to take within a certain period of time. Review it on a regular basis. If you are not progressing toward that goal, ask yourself why. Writing down your goals cannot be overemphasized. I have a work basket in my home office with the words, "Stop dreaming and start doing." At this writing, I am progressively working on finishing a number of books I have been working on for a while. I used to forget about them until I created goals for their completion. Admittedly, life sometimes gets in your way, but you have to keep adjusting your schedule until they are finished. Discipline is required. Sometimes that means not watching television or doing other things. When people make excuses for not starting a business or doing other things, I want to ask how many hours do you spend watching television a day. Enough said.

Additionally, don't find yourself in your forties and fifties and not have a backup plan. If you say you are stuck and in a rut, my question is, what are you doing about it? I am stunned every time I hear people say outside of corporate America, they have no other interests. While working in corporate America, I started a church, Cathedral of Faith International Ministries; started my personal ministry, Gwen Wheeler International Ministries; wrote books; dreamed about starting a floral business, and took floral designing courses. Hanging upon my cubicle was a picture of a florist shop that reminded me that I had something else to do. That picture is framed and hanging on my home office wall. When I retired, I enrolled into a floral designing school, Rittners School of Floral Design, Boston, Massachusetts, and graduated. After graduation, I started my floral designing business, Sensational Floral Designs by Gwendolyn. Whew, that's a lot, but I live a full life and don't miss corporate America at all. I chose not to allow them to define or limit me nor make me invisible. Yet understand that every business I started and every book I wrote had a starting point. Nothing is accomplished without a plan or goal in place.

Incidentally, I gave some advice earlier that I want to repeat here: Please don't walk through the corporate halls with your eyes and ears closed. Betrayers give off signals, but don't let them know you know. Devise a plan of response that works best for you and your career. Then execute your plan in a professional manner. Your plan of success is in your hands. Manage it.

With this in mind, pay attention to the changes made that affects you and understand corporate philosophy. For example, if they put an incompetent manager over you or one that insults your intelligence every day, treat that as a wake-up call. When corporate America doesn't have a good reason to fire you or eliminate your job, they try to aggravate you greatly so that you will quit. My advice to you is don't quit unless you have a plan or some place to go. Don't hurt yourself. If they want you to leave, I have two words for them: severance package.

As an illustration about devising a successful plan, I want to tell you one of my favorite stories about a young Black woman named Alison. She was doing a great job and was qualified to be a senior person on her team. However, her boss's perception was different from hers, so she told Alison that she wasn't ready. Have you heard that excuse before? The invisible syndrome was at work again. Alison came to work every day with a smile on her face and continued to do a good job. Her smiling face and positive attitude kept them from suspecting that she was looking for another job. You can guess how this story turned out, but you need me to fill in the details. Alison not only obtained a senior representative position with another company but the new company offered her $10,000 more a year than she was presently making. With this senior position came an office and other fringe benefits. Ah, success is the best revenge. Alison is a Christian who knew the importance of trusting God to empower her not only to recover from a boss with a poor perception of her but to reach beyond that perception and obtain a better job.

Then there was a man we will call Adam, who worked in the accounting department at the Water Storage Company. He was an accounting clerk who went back to school to get his bachelor's degree. Before he finished his degree program, he met with the controller of the company to see what opportunities would be available for him after graduation. The controller told him nothing would be available. This was not a racial, prejudicial decision because Adam was Caucasian. He just didn't fit their image of what a manager should look like and wasn't a part of the clique. His work was valuable to this company, but they didn't want to promote him. Adam did not allow their perception of him to place limitations on his life or destroy his dream of advancing. Like Alison, he reached beyond management's perception of him and got a better job. They didn't know he was looking for other employment because he would just call in sick or say he had a doctor's appointment when he had interviews. They were shocked when he actually got another job. This invisible man became visible simply by daring to leave his comfort zone and step outside the doors of a company he had worked at for years.

Sexual Harassment

As I write this section, it is October 2017. Allegations of sexual misconduct, rape, sexual harassment in the workplace are flooding the news, internet, Twitter, Facebook, and I am sure other social media outlets. The obvious question by some is why the victims waited so many years before coming forward and joining the MeToo Movement. That question can be answered easily by women who worked in corporate America in the 1970s. Back then, the term *sexual harassment* was not widely known. Women had no real voice in corporate America. In fact, I was shocked to read this: "Cornell University activists coined the term sexual harassment in 1975, and this pervasive problem was finally given a name. Public awareness of the issue has risen since then."

Frankly, I worked in Personnel during that time, and I never saw that term come across my desk. Yet I know that problem existed because I encountered it. The coined term *sexual harassment* wasn't a well-known legal term. In fact, we talked about these uncomfortable situations among ourselves. This was a problem we felt could not be resolved through Personnel. Some of it was blatant, and other times it appeared in the form of lustful looks and creepy smiles. Here are some examples.

- A man we will call Wayne Jones is one of the reasons I started wearing suit jackets. One afternoon I walked into his office where he was conducting a meeting attended by all men. His eyes started roaming my upper body. That was so humiliating. At that time we didn't address sexual harassment. Who was I going to report him to? He was the VP of Personnel. That was the last opportunity he had to undress me with his eyes. I purchased jackets and wore them daily. This same man propositioned a friend I will call Melinda. At an office Christmas party, he asked her, "How far do you want to go in the company?" She turned down the offer. If she had accepted his offer, I was going to educate her on the fact that that man had no real power to help her. He was just a figurehead and probably not worth the money they paid him. I heard he was great when negotiating with the unions.
- Sexual harassment comes from all levels. One of the mail room clerks had an annoying habit of touching me. I

tried discreetly to stop him from touching me. When that didn't work, I threatened to break his arm. That dramatic approach didn't work either. One day he came over to my desk, with his married self, put his arms around me, put his chin on my head, and said, "Your hair smells nice." Shortly after that I was standing in the hall, and he put his arm around me. That pushed me over the edge, so in the middle of the office, I screamed, "Get your hands off my body!" He ran, and I never had another problem with him. A thought just came to mind: nobody came out of their office to see what I was screaming about. That was sad. Maybe they were afraid to find out who was touching me. I refused that day to be a perpetual victim. It was bad enough I had to tolerate that from a vice president and even one of my managers.

- That leads me to my next incident. I walked into one of my manager's office one day with a knit dress on, and he couldn't keep his eyes off me. He just kept staring at me without saying a word. My older brother had to educate me on how men look at women. My naive self kept buying the wrong dresses because I thought I looked nice, but I had to get corporate smart and buy different-type attire. Instead of looking like a sexy young lady, I started looking like an older business woman. Clearly, I hear you saying, "You should have been able to dress the way you wanted." I agree with you, but I was uncomfortable and felt violated. My change of clothing kept those dirty men from drooling over a twenty-year-old woman's body. Was I flattered by their attention? No, I was annoyed, but again we couldn't just walk into the Personnel office back then and file a report like people do today.

- Another incident occurred that I am not sure what to call it, so I am going to put it in this section. One day I was sitting at the receptionist desk, and the president of the company asked me to do something related to business. Then he in turn lift his belt up for me to see his buckle. That didn't make sense to me then or even now. Why would I want to look at your buckle? That really made me uncomfortable. I didn't know what he was up to when he lifted his belt.

In later years, sexual harassment was no longer acceptable in the workplace. This is how they defined it: "Sexual advances, whether they involve physical touching or not; leering, whistling, brushing against an individual's body, making sexual gestures or comments; inquiries into one sexual experiences." The company's policy is clear on this: "Such conduct will not be tolerated,"

A Roadblock to Success

A Job that Never Occurred

After retiring from corporate America, a short time later I ran into some financial difficulties. For that reason, I decided to return to work. I interviewed with a prominent hospital in Boston, and it seemed to be a good fit. The salary and benefits were exceptional, and I got excited about the possibility of getting out of the financial hole I was in. However, the hospital's hiring process had one final step: previous managers and coworkers had to fill out and submit references electronically to the hospital's human resources. This involved them giving me a rating in different categories and adding any additional comments.

Frankly, I expected the next phone conversation from HR to be "Congratulations, you have the job and we expect you to report to work on a specific date." Unfortunately, one of the people I thought would give me a good reference failed to do so. At least I think it was one person, but I don't really know. We don't always know people as well as we think we do. When the unexpected happened, I was shocked that the HR rep at the hospital called to tell me they decided to go with someone else. What? Our last conversation indicated that I was the candidate they wanted, and the references were just a formality, so I thought. Immediately, I started questioning her as to what happened. My intuition was telling me someone betrayed me. At first she was reluctant to tell me, but I pressured her and said, "I have a right to know if someone gave me a negative reference." She wouldn't say who, but she indicated someone had and added the comment, "I thought you would have chosen people you trusted." That left me speechless. Incidentally, I thought I had chosen trusted colleagues, and if they didn't feel comfortable in giving me a positive reference, they should have refused. My past work experience with them did not warrant them writing a negative reference. Even though we may have had a different opinion now and then, my work record demonstrated the exceptional work I did that made a difference in the company. As a result of their unfortunate decision, their comments not only prevented me from obtaining that position but any other position at that hospital. In other words, I was placed on a do-not-hire list. To this day I still don't understand what I did to someone to make them block a job opportunity.

Moreover, I was going to either find out who blocked me or leave a clear message to all that this was unacceptable behavior. No doubt the person who gave the negative reference did not expect HR to tell me about it. As my brother, Michael, said, "They didn't expect you to shake down the HR person and get an answer." By the way, one of my nicknames is Dick Tracy. He was an American comic who was a tough and intelligent police detective. I contacted every person I had used as a reference and told them I didn't get the job because one of them gave me a bad reference. In the most dramatic way possible, I asked them, "Why would you consent to being a reference if you were not going to say something positive?" Further, I tried my best to make them feel guilty about how bad I needed this job.

Responses started coming back quickly. Everyone responded except for the main person I had worked with. Most of my experiences with her had been good, but we did have a couple of incidents over the years. Yet when we departed, I thought we were good. If I had suspected any bad blood existed between us, I wouldn't have listed her as my manager. In fact, when she transferred to a different department, I helped her move files and clean her desk out. That was an act of friendship because I had a new boss and was not required to help her. Also, I had lunch with her when she retired from that company, and she hugged me as a friend would. The Temptations sang a song that said, "Smiling faces sometimes pretend to be your friend. Smiling faces show no traces of the evil that lurks within. Smiling faces, smiling faces sometimes they don't tell the truth." So again, I don't understand why.

In an attempt to make me feel better about this incident, one of my former colleagues wrote, "Gwen, this may not make sense to you right now, but maybe this wasn't the place you were supposed to be. My mother didn't get a job one time, and the person who got it was miserable." At that time, I didn't want to hear that because I was angry that I had been betrayed. Although Romans 8:28 was ringing out in my ear, "And we know that all things work together for good to those who love God, to those who are the called according to His purpose." The job I applied for was a receptionist job that required me to be at work at 7:30 a.m., and I would support two managers whom I had not met because the office manager made the decision.

To be honest, that would not have been the best fit for me, because I am not a morning person. If I have to talk with people that early in the morning, it would be very stressful. In addition, getting there before 7:30 a.m. was definitely going to be a challenge, especially during a winter snowstorm in Boston. Besides, the office manager wasn't a joke. She probably wouldn't have accepted any excuse for being late. Although I had my reservations about accepting this position, the money and benefits were very appealing, and I was desperate.

Other opportunities came up, and even though I had the skills and experience, I was unable to get a job. Eventually I decided it was time for me to take a leap of faith and not return to work.

Ultimately, whatever you do, make a note to yourself to be happy, healthy, and at peace. Find ways to celebrate your own success in healthy ways. Buy yourself some flowers, a plaque, or a trophy. Take a trip or budget for that outfit that makes you feel like Mister or Miss Success. Please don't waste another minute being depressed about a supervisor or coworker who does not have the proper perception to see how valuable you are.

Moreover, don't stop being your best self because you don't feel appreciated. Being your best is the best gift you can give to yourself. During a performance evaluation, Rosy said to me, "Gwen, you have high standards not because I require it of you but because you require it of yourself." That job is temporary, and one day all that once seemed so overwhelming will be merely shadows in your mind. The invisible syndrome will no longer be a part of your life. Names and faces will fade, but the results of that character-building process will remain forever. You are very visible, my friend! Let's celebrate that fact!

CHAPTER 3

· · · ●●●●● · · ·

My Wounded Comrades

In the previous chapter I wrote about the devastation of pain and change and how they fostered the invisible syndrome. Much of what I have written about has been about my own personal pain. Now I want to share some stories about other wounded corporate comrades. As usual, their names have been changed. This chapter is their platform to speak their truth and tell their story.

First, we must understand that wounds can be physical, emotional, or psychological. However, in this chapter, we will focus on emotional and psychological wounds. Alas, they are more difficult to identify and heal. Too often these wounds are hidden behind smiles, a resolve to survive, destructive habits, obnoxious gestures, and machismo.

For emphasis and clarity, I grouped some of their stories according to similarities.

Alcohol Addiction

In my opinion, corporate America rarely sympathizes with emotional pain. Therefore, employees try to mask their pain sometimes in destructive ways. Consuming too much alcohol is one of the destructive ways people use to cover their pain. There were three employees within the same company that had drinking problems. The history of why they became addicted to this substance is unknown to me. National Council on Alcoholism and Drug Dependence gave these facts about alcohol:

- Alcohol is the most commonly used addictive substance in the United States: 17.6 million people, or one in every 12 adults, suffer from alcohol abuse or dependence along with several million more who engage in risky, binge drinking patterns that could lead to alcohol problems.
- More than half of all adults have a family history of alcoholism or problem drinking, and more than 7 million children live in a household where at least one parent is dependent on or has abused alcohol.
- Alcohol abuse and alcoholism can affect all aspects of a person's life. Long-term alcohol use can cause serious health complications, can damage emotional stability, finances, career, and impact one's family, friends, and community.

It's only by the grace of God that so many of us have escaped the grasp of this predator. Here are their stories.

- The first of these stories is about a man we will call Frank, who was a sales director. There were days he would not show up for work, and we didn't know where he was. At least I didn't know where he was. He would sometimes go into his office and close the door for no obvious reason. Later they found the bottles of liquor in his cabinet. The company finally persuaded or demanded him to go into rehabilitation. His drinking problem caused him to be demoted from the position of sales director.
- When Frank returned from rehabilitation, he had been demoted to a sales representative. Sadly, he still had a drinking problem. One of the signs that he still had a problem was that he would lose things such as reports. In his meetings with the director, he would tell him he had given them to me, and I didn't know where they were. By this

time, a stronger personality had emerged out of me, so I was not about to take the blame for his inability to remember where he put things. One day he asked me to look for one of those lost documents. Those words were spoken in a tone I didn't like. I said, "Okay, but I know you didn't give it to me." My assertiveness shocked them. Later I discovered that my response was considered to be negative behavior. Really? You knew this man had a drinking problem. Undoubtedly you weren't trained on how to help him, and I didn't have training either. As my manager, you should have taken me aside and told me how to handle his accusations better. Was I supposed to allow myself to become the scapegoat and let him make me feel incompetent?

- Thinking back, maybe his memory was foggy because of the alcohol, and he sincerely believed he gave me those documents. Did my director believe he gave me the reports? Frankly, management finds it easier to believe that we are the incompetent ones. Leadership supports leadership, right or wrong. On the other hand, was he trying to save face at my expense, not expecting me to defend myself? Obviously, I came to my own conclusion and decided not to be the scapegoat.

- Regrettably, this story did not end well. Frank died while swimming. It didn't make sense that he had drowned because he was an excellent swimmer. Rumors spread through the company that alcohol was the suspected culprit for this accidental drowning.

- The next story is about a woman we will call Ruby. Ruby was the receptionist with an alcohol addiction. We had a PA system that was used when urgent phone calls came in and the person's whereabouts was unknown. I hated to hear those announcements when I was in the ladies' room. It felt like an invasion of privacy. Most of the day those announcements were clear, then around three o'clock her voice became slurred. She became more obnoxious. Let's not discuss the office Christmas parties.

- Being one of her backup reliefs was one of my job assignments. One day I observed a cup of unknown substance on her desk. I asked, "What's that?" She responded, "It's tea." A funny color for tea, and it was cold. That mistake didn't occur again. HR never challenged that behavior, which is sad, because she needed help. After I left the company, a new company took it over. Ruby was no longer the receptionist.

- Our third story is about a man we will call Hunter. Hunter was the national sales director who saw too many younger guys being promoted—some had once reported to him. On a sales trip he had one too many drinks at the bar. Two unsavory characters watched him and followed him back to his hotel room. The intoxication prevented him from rationally being able to decide what to do when someone you don't know knocks at your door. They told him they were room service. Hunter had not ordered room service but still opened the door to these two men. These thugs beat him up and left him in the bathtub. Rumor was he didn't have that much money on him, because credit cards were the primary way he paid for sales trips.

- When he came back to work, his eye was still black from where he had been beaten. Thankfully they didn't kill him, and he did survive physically, but emotionally he was never the same. How would you like your coworkers to know you were so drunk that you let robbers into your room, which should have been a place of sanctuary? That happened over thirty years ago, but I am still cautious when I stay at a hotel, especially if I am by myself. In fact, I am cautious at home. I have a security camera in which I can look at from my phone. If the wrong person shows up on my doorsteps, I don't even respond. One guy was waving at the camera for me to open the door. Another guy yelled and said, "Open the door!" I yelled back, "No!"

The Revolving Door

Sales Department

The invisible syndrome shows up in the form of employees being laid off. Yet a greater volume seemed to occur within the sales department. A revolving door symbolizes how quickly people came and left. Within my thirty-seven years of corporate experience, I worked for two different sales companies, a total of over twenty years combined. As the sales assistant, I had the unpleasant task of cleaning out workstations after sales staff left the company. Their files were transferred to others, and anything that could not become recycled supplies was thrown away. A spirit of depression seemed to linger when they left. It felt like a graveyard filled with broken lives and broken dreams.

Reaching sales quotas was the basis for a long-term sales career. When those goals were unmet after a certain period of time, sales-people quietly walked out the door without any fanfare. Farewell parties were a rarity. It was understood that the success and longevity of our company depended on these risk-takers making quota. The rules were not always fair, and people were not treated equally. Here are some of their stories.

- A woman we will call Minnie was a person you either loved or hated. She had a personality that was difficult to find a middle ground. Minnie's director passionately and openly despised her. One day I openly heard her director say, "I am going to pin her—to the wall." You can fill in that space. Minnie jokingly said to me, "At least at this company, you know who is hacking you." We laughed. When she saw the handwriting on the wall that indicated they were getting ready to fire her, she went back to her previous employer and got her job back. Minnie was a smart woman and resigned before they could fire her. We celebrated and cheered her on.

- Similarly, a woman we will call Katie wasn't liked either. From the surface she looked disgruntled and unorganized. Yet when I heard she was leaving the company, I felt sorry for her. Sometimes words escape you. There is no easy way to say, "I am sorry you are being laid off." Instead, I said, "I am sorry you are leaving." Shortly after her departure, I bumped into Katie on the street. She said, "I couldn't tell you then, but I already had another job before I left." She laughed and said, "I am collecting two paychecks." Good for her.

- A familiar cliché says, "What goes around comes around." The past director of Minnie and Katie was laid off a year or two later. She didn't even say goodbye. We came in one Monday morning, and her office was cleared out. Her corner glass office was noticeably empty. The reason for her departure was never discussed.

- Then there was the time a man we will call Mack experienced the invisible syndrome in a different way. He was a salesperson who was not only a company man but he was very well-liked. I can still see him coming through the doors of the sales office with a smile on his face. The Water Storage Company had what they called the Silver Club, which was for retirees who were with the company for at least twenty-five years. Mack was looking forward to being a part of that elite club upon his retirement because they were given great benefits. Then the unexpected occurred: one year before he reached his twenty-fifth year with the company, he was forced to retire. They did not make any exceptions. His heart was broken because he would not be able to join other fellow retirees who were members of the Silver Club. Without a doubt, new leadership showed up who did not perceive Mack as being valuable. He ended his career in an invisible state. Hopefully, he was able to bounce back from that disappointment.

- Finally, when people retire, you hope they will have a long, happy, and prosperous retirement. Such was not the case for a man we will call Barry. Barry was one of my favorite guys, a pleasure to work for. Shortly after his retirement, he had a heart attack and died. His wife found him lying across his bed with a black box in his hand. It seems he was looking for something. So sad.

Fragile Egos and Mishaps

When egos are allowed to go unchecked in the workplace, the invisible syndrome is allowed to foster. Thus, many good employees have been let go or denied promotions because their bosses had a fragile ego. That fragile ego clouded their perception and caused them to make wrong decisions. As I wrote in chapter 2, "People's perception determines how bosses evaluate and interact with you. Although you are the same person, two bosses can see you differently." Some stories follow.

- Timmy wrote a personal blog about his incompetent, arrogant, and rude boss. With one mistaken click, he sent this link to the boss. After reading the blog, although his name wasn't mentioned, his boss knew he was the man being described. The company could not discipline him for writing the blog, but it was transmitted through company's property and perceived as being written during work hours. He was placed on probation for inappropriately using company's property. Needless to say, the tension increased between the two of them. I left the company before Timmy, and hopefully my departure inspired him to pursue another job. The vice president, who sat in on that ridiculous meeting, asked Timmy why he was leaving. Don't know what answer he gave, but I made it plain why I was leaving. He should have told him to read between the lines. Karma eventually caught up with Timmy's boss. He was laid off a couple of years later, but not before he had destroyed a few other careers.

- Sometimes invisibility manifests itself in ways that are not always obvious. For example, Karen got tired of being ignored by senior leaders as she walked down the hollow halls. It bothered her when they would look pass her and not speak. Their apparent lack of acknowledgment made her feel invisible. I used the word *apparent* because I am not sure they saw her. They might have just had other things on their mind. I, on the other hand, didn't care if they spoke to me or not. That wasn't important to me and didn't define me. Yet that was important to Karen, so she decided to really become visible. She left the company to open her own bakery shop. Her business was successful, and we missed all those tasty desserts she used to bring to work. Apple pie was one of my favorites. Instead of baking me a cake for my birthday, she baked me an apple pie.

- In chapter 1 I wrote, "When people don't value you, they can make you invisible." Further, I wrote, "People try and make other people feel invisible for various reasons."

- Certainly, we have no control over what people say or do, but we can choose how we will respond to their actions. As I said before, "Your plan of success is in your hands. Manage it." Moreover, manage it well. Please don't make an emotional, illogical decision. My next story saddens me as I think about how a woman we will call Terry chose to manage an invisibility situation that she encountered.

- In the beginning, we used humor as a way to handle this invisibility. We laughed at the evaluation numbers we were given. Our response was "I know I am a 5 [highest] although they gave me a 3 [in-between]." We were each other's support system. Although we both had enough of the nonsense in our department, we both handled it differently. My solution was to ask for a transfer into the Sales Department, taking two of my bosses with me. My move was a lateral one.

- However, Terry decided on a different course of action, which I still don't understand today. She asked to be transferred into the mail room as a mail clerk. Frankly, there is nothing wrong with working in the mail room, but she was on a higher grade. Her job was equivalent to an assistant manager's position. She allowed the invisible syndrome game playing to make her request a transfer that was a demotion down a few grades. I can still see her taking her box to the mail room. No leader in that company stood up for this woman who had worked so hard for the company. That saddens me.

- Generally, employees are expected to be flexible and to take on more responsibility when asked. Leaders are always expecting their subordinates to grow in their jobs. That's a fair expectation. On the other hand, they don't necessarily want to pay more money or promote them. That's not fair. Both parties should get something out of this. Jessica decided the leaders in her division were taking too long, so she went to HR and had them evaluate her job. HR agreed with Jessica—that was a miracle. Her HR rep determined the level of her job should be raised. Her leaders weren't happy that she went over their heads. At review time, they punished her by lowering her ranking mark. Her job hadn't changed and the level of expertise she brought to the job hadn't changed. The change was on paper. When she questioned her leader, she was told because her job was new. Can you say baloney? Jessica didn't accept that explanation and refused to allow them to make her invisible. She decided it was time to move on, and she did exactly that. Her next position was a higher one.

- In time, Jessica's manager faced an invisibility event herself. Be careful how you treat others, because it might come back to you in bad Karma. Let's call her Leticia. Drake became her boss after the restructuring of the division. You remember Drake, right? Drake was made vice president. Leticia had been at the company longer than Drake. She was not happy when they promoted him over her. Was he more qualified than her? No, he was a recipient of the Ron fan network. Yes, Ron was a part of this invisible syndrome again. In corporate America, sometimes how high you go is determined by how much you can kiss up and stroke a person's ego. That is why Drake was so arrogant and rude.

- Managers, directors, and vice presidents who are not properly trained are the worst leaders. They can be obnoxious and degrading. One day I heard him say to her, "What's the matter? You don't look happy." Really, Einstein? I just wanted to slap him and say, "Do you know why she is looking that way? She has worked hard for years in this company, and she is rewarded by having to work for a jerk like you." The person who reported to Leticia couldn't take the change. He was a young guy, so he easily moved on to his next career path. There was tension between Drake and Leticia. He wasn't happy that Leticia wasn't thrilled about working for him. She made the mistake of confiding in Ron because they had worked together longer and she thought they were friends. Ron was up to his old tricks and told Drake about the conversation. They laid her off. Others I knew were also let go on a bogus charge. My attitude would have been negatively affected by this nonsense, and I am glad that I was not around to see this unfold.

By the way, Karma eventually caught up to Ron. His boss retired, and the new boss had his own staff. Ron was given another less impressive position. He eventually retired and had the nerve to say he wasn't treated right. Really? One of the scriptures that describe your exit is found in Galatians 6:7, "Be not deceived; God is not mocked: for whatsoever a man soweth, that shall he also reap." Another scripture declares, "Beloved, do not avenge yourselves, but rather give place to wrath; for it is written, 'Vengeance is Mine, I will repay,' says the Lord." Ron had wronged many people, including me.

To summarize some of those shenanigans, he was responsible for my demotion when I worked for David, plotted to get me fired when I no longer wanted to work for Greg, and while working for Drake, doubled as a spy. One night he walked boldly into my cubicle and looked at my computer to see what I was working on. Rumors were probably circulating that I was working on another book, and I was. Yet I am not going to stay late at work when I knew he is in his office and work on it. Then he would stand outside my cubicle, in back where a file cabinet was located, and pretend he was reading articles, watching me. I wanted to say, "You really would be more comfortable reading those articles at your desk rather than standing at my file cabinet." Would I really work on something personal when I know you are close enough to see what I am doing? How many times did that man go to the bathroom a day, walking by my cubicle? In spite of all his evil plots, the scripture that sums up my relationship with him and the victorious outcome of my journey is, "'No weapon formed against you shall prosper, And every tongue which rises against you in judgment You shall condemn. This is the heritage of the servants of the Lord, And their righteousness is from Me,' Says the Lord" (Isaiah 54:17). I left that company as a visible woman on my own terms with money in my bank account and a smile on my face.

- Unfortunately, I have one more victim of Ron's evil plots to write about. His partner in crime was Rosy. She had an evil side as well, which I also encountered later on. A woman we will call Patty had done her job well for years and had raving reviews. Again, a new boss, which happened to be Rosy, came, and tension developed. The main issue Patty struggled with was that her new manager was not as qualified as she was. Rosy even told me that Patty was better at her job than she was. The letting go of Patty was a process and a continual drama that unfolded. There were bad performance reviews and low bonuses given to her. They worked hard at making her feel invisible. The signs that they were building a false case against her were flashing neon lights.

- One time Patty was so upset that she just wanted to throw in the towel and quit. Immediately I turned into corporate advisor and told her, "Don't quit! If you quit, you will not receive any type of financial compensation. Take some days off and don't make an emotional decision." She took my advice. That day I wanted to say more, but I wasn't sure if she was ready to hear the rest of my advice. When the handwriting is clearly on the wall that plans could be in place to eliminate your job, get you a plan. Don't wait for them to make their move. Patty didn't have a plan in place.

- One afternoon we were taking our walk, and Patty suddenly stopped. She looked at us and said, "I think I am being let go today, because I have a meeting with Ron and Rosy at three thirty." Immediately, we went into the supportive mode and tried to assure her that maybe she was just being paranoid. My experience at InfoData seemed so far in the pass that I forgot it was four o'clock in the afternoon when I was told my job was eliminated. The difference is Jack was being sneaky and wanted me to finish the projects I was working on.

- Patty's premonition was correct. She was escorted to the conference room at three thirty, and an HR rep was waiting there. Ron and Rosy walked away. When Patty came back to her desk, she packed her box and told me the disturbing news: her position was eliminated. Knowing that walk to leave the building could be a lonely one, I went down the elevator with her and then walked her to the door. My heart was saddened. That day she exited from this particular melodrama called corporate games. Before making her exit, she left an imprint that would remind them that this woman, whom they tried hard to make invisible, was really very visible. Rosy needed the articles that Patty had been working on to complete her projects. She gave me the task of finding those files, which I was unable to locate. When I told her I couldn't find those files, a startled look came on her face as she spoke these words, "She deleted the files." Touché! Patty decided they were not going to profit from her hard work. Since my job is eliminated, I am going to eliminate the files that could help you.

- In retrospect, I am sure that is the reason so many companies do not allow employees to return to their workstations or cubicles. When my job was eliminated at InfoData, I was so tempted to send what we called a worldwide message, which would read, "This is how they treat employees who have been loyal to the company. They eliminated my job." Thankfully, I took the high road and left quietly until I regrouped and sent my complaint through the proper channels.

- At times my journey through corporate America crossed paths with people I didn't know—they were a name recorded on a tape. Those occurrences happened when I worked in the Personnel Department at the Water Storage Company. Paul had to travel to other locations and interact with employees. Those interactions had to be recorded for legal purposes, and I had to type them. One particular tape I listened to made me angry. A woman was being interviewed who was on Valium, and Paul was trying to use this against her. Somehow I believe her job was probably the reason she was on Valium. If it wasn't for the grace of God, so many of us would be on Valium or addicted to alcohol like the other comrades I mentioned. The comment recorded at the end really bothered me. Paul said, "And then she cried." A few days later, papers arrived stating that she voluntarily resigned. I thought to myself, I bet she did. Hopefully, that woman received some sort of financial compensation. He would not have bullied me out of a job. They find vulnerable people to prey on and then come back to the office with smiles on their faces.

- Another part of my job that I actually hated while working in Personnel was managing the process of typing performance evaluations for the whole company. By this time, a more professional system was in place that required employees to review and sign them. Directors and managers were no longer allowed to write and file secret, false evaluations without reviewing it with the employees.

- While typing evaluations one day, I started saying out loud, "Lies, lies." That was a sure sign it was time to make a change. All employees were not evaluated according to their performance. Sometimes the personalities didn't mesh. Paul said to me at the beginning of this process, "I don't have to tell you, but you know this is confidential." No kidding! At that point it was time for me to get a transfer, and as stated earlier, I received one.

Our experiences through corporate America may differ. The degree of our pain and loss may not be the same. Yet remember the words I wrote earlier. "Certainly, we have no control over what people say or do, but we can choose how we will respond to their actions. Your plan of success is in your hands. Manage it. Moreover, manage it well. Please don't make an emotional, illogical decision."

CHAPTER 4

· · · ◆ ◆ ◆ ◆ · · ·

Funny Corporate Stories with a Twist of Aggravation

In chapter 3, I wrote about using humor as a means of dealing with the invisible syndrome. Humor is a necessary tool that will help you survive corporate drama. Learning to find humorous nuggets along your journey to success will preserve your sanity. It doesn't have to always be a full-blown laugh. Sometimes a smile will suffice. A sticker read, "Smile often for the fun of it." Besides, you may diffuse potential explosive situations with a smile. Smiling will throw folks off guard and cause them to back off.

Sometimes people are intimidated by your smile or pleasant disposition. Consequently, they try to think of ways to make you miserable so they can get the smile off your face. It is an evil control game they play. Yet you take all the power and fun out of their game when you smile or laugh.

A woman we will call Shirley was a receptionist for the executive suite. She always had this big smile on her face that would light up a room. One day, a person, who should not have been a supervisor in the first place, said some negative things to her during her performance evaluation. Then she stood back, hoping her smile would fade. Her supervisor had the nerve to say to her, "Let's see if you keep that smile on your face." Shirley looked at the picture of her son on her desk. That reminded her why she kept smiling and tolerating such shenanigans. She was working to take care of him, so she kept smiling.

The following are some additional corporate stories with both humor and aggravation mixed together.

Corporate Friendship

The invisible syndrome can be perpetuated by a friend. Friendship is one of those funny oddities with some twists and turns. It can embrace and lift you up one moment and slam you to the floor a few minutes later. Such was the friendship between Terry and I. Some days she was my listening ear and a shoulder to cry on. Further, she was the birthday party organizer who decorated your cubicle and made sure you had plenty of goodies, flowers, and presents to open. The white-and-gold cup she gave me for my thirtieth birthday still sits in my kitchen hutch. She had a sense of humor that would cheer you up and save your sanity. There are birthday cards I still have in an old scrapbook. One year she gave me a framed picture of a secretary in a starting position to run out the door with a mouse holding a gun to signal when it was time to go home. The clock read 4:59, and the phone was ringing off the hook. That picture didn't depict me, because I was always the one staying late to finish a project. Yet it made me laugh, and I carried it with me from office to office and job to job.

On other days, I questioned if she was my friend or enemy. So many sarcastic and mean-spirited comments I let slide by without a response. Somehow deep within, I knew she was a hurting person who, hopefully unintentionally, hurt other people, including her friends. That's the truth I choose to believe as I share some of those comments. When I got promoted to the personnel secretary, Terry did not say congratulations. Instead, she said, "Ron only promoted you because he needed a minority in his department." Wow, that hurt. She tried to devalue me that day, yes, make me feel invisible. According to her, my hard work, experience, professionalism, and secretarial and administrative skills had nothing to do with being chosen for such a prestigious position. Thankfully, I knew better.

Another time I told her about a young, handsome, intelligent executive who wanted to marry me. More darts were thrown at me. She said, "I thought he would want to marry someone really pretty." Come on now, those of you who're reading this have to laugh at that statement. I am smiling as I am remembering those words. Well, he thought I was beautiful outwardly and inwardly. In fact, he pursued me for many years. Finally, I made him understand that God made it plain I could not marry him. Then he left me alone. Thankfully, I listened because his story didn't end well. That's all I will say about that.

Then there was the annoying habit she had of paging me when I was in the bathroom. It was never about a business call, but it would be about a personal call. The words would ring out over the PA system, "Gwen, you have a phone call. It's personal." Those aren't the words you want everybody in the office to hear, especially not your boss. Unless it was an emergency, and it never was, she could send it into my voice mail. Certainly I could call them back.

So why did we remain friends until her untimely death? There were elements of our friendship that were worth holding onto, and I felt she needed my friendship. We did have some good times together. Terry's life had some disappointing events. Her disappointments included a failed marriage and failed career. For the most part, she was miserable. Although I am not a therapist, I think miserable people have the tendency to try and make other people miserable. Yet I know she cared about me, and I cared about her. Ultimately, I didn't allow those irritating and questionable friendship moments to destroy our friendship. That was a choice I'll never regret.

The Race Is On

Who Will Win Today?

While working in Personnel at the Water Storage Company, I reported primarily to Paul. He was very much of an early-morning person. Rising and arriving early has been a lifelong struggle for me, even now. If I had my choice, I would have preferred to arrive later in the morning and leave later in the evening. As long as I got the work done, why should it matter what time I got there?

However, Paul was a stickler when it came to punctuality. I was confused at first about what on time for work meant according to his standards. On time to me meant checking in before 9:00 a.m. and being across the hall getting a cup of coffee. That misunderstanding was quickly cleared up one morning. My friend, Terry, came looking for me and said Paul was looking for me. It was only a few minutes after nine o'clock, and I was in the building, so I didn't see what the big deal was. Paul in a very unpleasant and stern voice said to me, "When I come looking for you at nine o'clock, I want to find you somewhere around your desk." Terry and I had visions of me sitting on top of the file cabinet with coffee in hand with a smile on my face. That would be considered somewhere around my desk. Don't worry, I didn't live out that vision.

As a matter of fact, that was the day the race between Paul and me began. Who would get to my desk in the morning was the challenge of the day. Picture this, on a late, rainy morning, I could be seen running through the doors, rollers still in my hair and a scarf on. Thankfully, my office was located near the door. Paul's office was located further away, but exactly 9:00 a.m., unless he was in a meeting, you could hear the steps of this tall, heavyset man coming rapidly down the hall heading toward my office. It didn't matter if rollers were still in my hair. If I beat him to the desk, I won the race for that morning. The quiet silence of that victory was always overwhelmed by his ear-piercing morning salutation, "GOOD MORNING!" That's how it sounded to me. If we were tied or he won, a big smile would be on his face.

Penciled In

I Didn't Mean What I Wrote!

One of the most dreaded events in corporate America is performance evaluation time. Most of the stuff written is either a matter of your boss's perception or a justification for the raise percentage leadership decided across the board. Generally, those evaluations are written in ink or typed. My first performance evaluation with Paul was undoubtedly an experimental one. It was written in pencil. Overall the evaluation was okay, but he wrote two comments that bothered me. Following are those comments:

- Wayne Jones said I misspelled a word *one time*. Clearly, this man had nothing of importance to contribute. Within a year's time, if I only misspelled a word one time, I think that is pretty good. That wasn't my response. In fact, I was really irritated when I said, "I know how to spell, and that was a typographic error. Did he have anything positive to say?" Incidentally, at that time in corporate history, we didn't have computers with spellcheckers. We had electronic typewriters, and we had to rely on our eyes to catch errors. If there was an error, we had to type something over. Paul must have told Wayne what I said because he tried to be nice to me the next time he saw me.

- Next he wrote that I was not assertive enough. Let me stop here and make this observation. When corporate America can't find any real negative remarks to make, they say you are not assertive enough or not proactive enough. But then if you are too outspoken, they say you have a chip on your shoulder. You are not approachable. You have an attitude problem. Again, I was irritated, so I spoke from my heart, "Look, I don't have a problem telling my bosses how I feel, but it is not professional." He immediately erased that remark.

Norma Rae Stood Up in Me

There are too many meetings held in corporate America, especially departmental ones. Don't know what got into me one day, but I decided to put myself on the agenda during one of our weekly meetings. It must have been performance evaluation time, and I had read something about the proper way to conduct a performance evaluation. So I passed out papers that outlined the proper way to evaluate—make positive remarks and not just negative ones. Paul was so nervous that his leg was shaking, and he said, "That is the way we do." I responded, "No, you don't." Terry thought I had finally had a breakdown. They called me Norma Rae after that meeting. For those of you who are not familiar with who Norma Rae was, she was a young, single mother and textile worker who agreed to help unionize her mill despite the problems and dangers involved. She fought for her coworkers like I was fighting for mine.

The Saga of Wayne Jones

Wayne had the reputation of disappearing during work hours. He reported to the president of the company. The president said jokingly to me one day, "Your primary responsibility is to know where Wayne Jones is at all times." That was an impossible task because Wayne would tell me he was going to the state where our paper mills were located, but he wasn't going to be at one of the mills. Moreover, he would say, "I can't be reached, but I will call in." Cell phones and pagers weren't available back then. If there was an emergency, you just hoped he would call in.

Allegedly, Wayne had girlfriends. One day a woman called when he was on the phone with someone else. She said, "Tell him I called, but I am not going to tell you what my name is, but he will know." Sure enough when I told him what this woman said, he knew who she was. By the way, did I tell you Wayne was married? I never met his wife, but somebody told me she had a drinking problem. Alas, he was probably the reason for this addiction.

Then one day an envelope came addressed to him and was marked "Personal." When I picked it up, it made noise like it had seeds in it. One day he left the seeds on top of his desk, and I couldn't resist the urge to see what kind of seeds they were. When I read the back of the package, it said these were fantasy seeds. It boasted that if you planted them, you could get a yacht, airplane, and other things.

While working for him, I received an education I had not applied for. Observing his behavior made me grow up and realize that just because he had the title of vice president didn't mean he had integrity. He was arrogant and not very diplomatic.

By accident, Wayne discovered another side of Gwen Wheeler that emerged while working for this company. The shy girl who joined Water Storage Company grew up. A strong, confident woman emerged, and I automatically stood up for myself. One morning I was very stressed because of all the work I had on my desk. He walked into my office, emptied a whole box of pencils on my desk, and said, "Sharpen these!" I didn't hear please or thank you. Approximately one hour later, he returned and asked me, "Did you sharpen my pencils?" I replied, "No, do you need them all now?" He said no and walked quickly out of my office and never asked me to sharpen another pencil. That day he made me angry, and I didn't care what title he had. Years later I laughed about how a twenty-plus-year-old woman stood up to one of the most powerful men in the company. Sometimes you just have had enough and the title of the person aggravating you loses its powerful meaning.

In essence, laughter is a sign of maturity. There are a lot of painful situations in corporate America that could destroy you, but don't let them. Instead, grow stronger through them and become more confident of yourself. Laugh at the audacity of those who think they have the power to destroy you. Find some way to laugh and laugh a lot.

CHAPTER 5

• • ♦ ♦ ● ♦ ♦ • •

The Conclusion

Putting the finishing touches on my portrait of thirty-seven years in corporate America was the goal of this book. However, as I began to reminisce and retrace my steps, a reality became apparent. My goal will not be achieved, because I decided not to tell the entire corporate story. To put it differently, some parts of the stories have purposely been left out so as not to bore you, while other parts are better left untold.

For the most part, I have shared a mixture of corporate stories, some sad and some happy. In life, there are no wasted experiences. In chapter 1, I wrote, "A professor told us that there should always be a learning process in everything we do." As a Christian, the foundation of my life is based on Romans 8:28, "And we know that all things work together for good to those who love God, to those who are the called according to His purpose." Ultimately, no matter how painful some of the events were, something good always came out of them. As a matter of fact, corporate America matured me and provided me with what we call transferrable skills.

When I began working in corporate America, I was a shy, quiet, naive, young woman. However, I walked out stronger, more confident, and visible with leadership skills. I started two nonprofit organizations: a church, Cathedral of Faith International Ministries, Inc., and personal ministry organization, Gwen Wheeler International Ministries, Inc. Then after graduating from Rittners School of Floral

Design in 2009, I started my floral design business, Sensational Floral Designs by Gwendolyn. In addition, this is my fifth published book, with many more to come.

While I worked in administrative positions, I learned how to multitask and how to use the various software applications right on the job. Sometimes I was provided formal training. Other times I wasn't. Nonetheless, I took advantage of every course offered, such as writing courses, communication courses, time management, Microsoft Office, etc. These skills have proven to be invaluable in helping me to be successful in all my endeavors. For that I am so grateful.

At this time, I would like to splash a ray of sunshine on my canvas of corporate experiences. There are four of my bosses that made my time at the Water Storage Company very special. The fifth person I will mention was a coworker and is still a friend today.

First, there was a man we will call Grayson. He was very personable, and the women loved him. I will spare you some of the messages I had to take. Grayson was a complicated man who had an eye for detail, and he was very nice to me. At Christmas one year, he gave me this silk scarf that I still have. Unlike other bosses, he didn't just pick up anything, but he noticed the colors in a dress I wore one day. That scarf reflected those colors. That spoke volumes to me that he cared enough to buy something I would like.

Secondly, another man we will call Nicholas. He didn't have the same eye like Grayson. Instead, he had his wife buy the gift. She just came right out and asked what I like because he was clueless. Nicholas and Grayson made sure they showed me appreciation on Secretaries' Day and Christmas. Yes, they were the ones who filled my desk with flowers and took me out for lunch.

Thirdly, another man we will call Benjamin was one of my favorite bosses. Benjamin was a sweetheart and a ray of sunshine in an environment that could be somewhat depressing. He was a mature gentleman who was ready for retirement. His wife had died, and he remarried. One day I gladly typed one paper for his new wife, and she acknowledged the fact that she knew it wasn't my job to type it for her. The whole family thought I was wonderful. For Christmas,

Benjamin and his wife wanted to take me and my husband or boyfriend to the opera with them. I had neither a husband nor boyfriend, so they gave me money instead. Before he retired, he said to me, "I don't need the money or the aggravation." Smart man—he got out while he was young enough to enjoy his life.

My fourth hero is a man we will call Richard. He was Benjamin's replacement and had one of the most powerful jobs in the company. Richard was feared by so many people. Yet he had a softer side, and the administrative staff loved him. The other leaders were jealous and shocked because we loved him so much. When I needed a reference for my new job opportunity, I ran quickly into his office and told him somebody was going to call him. I said, "Tell them how wonderful I am." He laughed and did exactly that. A lesser man or woman might have sabotaged my opportunity to advance. Thank you, Richard! As I was finishing this section, I googled to see if he was still around. Sadly, he passed in 2004.

Finally, my friend, I will call Heather. Heather was a true friend during my time I worked at a particular company. In fact, she still is my friend. I could always depend on her to tell the truth and keep my secrets. When I decided to leave that company, I told her about it. I wasn't sure how my appointment with HR would go. I wrote them a long letter about issues I was having with my young, arrogant manager. Frankly, I wanted some compensation for the emotional pain he had put me through. The details of that letter are intentionally left out. It has always been my intentions to keep the identity of people and places of employment veiled. This book was never meant to be an indictment. I just wanted to tell my story hoping it would help somebody else.

Before writing and delivering my letter to HR, I spent a week taking my personal things home little by little. Being careful to carry out my secret mission after others had gone home was my plan. Mission was accomplished. A security guard saw me one night taking some things home. He just looked at me. No doubt he thought I had been fired.

There was one pink bin underneath my desk I wasn't able to take. I called Heather to tell her about the bin, and when no one was looking, she took it to her cubicle. Then she took it to her home until I could drive out there and get it. Someone else might have told other people, even though I said clearly don't tell. Yet in corporate America, I have had the opposite to happen. That job ended on my terms, and I received what I wanted. Heather is one of the few friendships I maintained after leaving a job. I love you, girl! Thank you for being my friend.

Without a doubt, there are different ways to define my thirty-seven years of corporate experience. For example, it can be compared to being on a journey. A journey defined means trip, voyage, ride, flight, passage, crossing, and excursion. In other words, we are traveling, moving from one place to another. None of us stay the same. There were many experiences and many people we met along the way. Some made us laugh, while others made us cry. One of the experiences we encountered was the invisible syndrome. As stated in chapter 1, one of the major lessons I learned was, when people don't value you, they can make you invisible. The word *value* means worth, importance, usefulness, appreciation, respect, and esteem. If anyone has ever tried to make you feel less than valuable, then they were treating you like you were invisible.

Another aspect of invisibility is criticism, but we can find value in criticism. Someone said, "There is a thread of truth in any criticism ever handed us. I want to learn from it, to grow, to allow my criticism to refine me, but not wash me out and beat me down." Further, don't allow others to validate you because their opinions change daily. Instead, connect with God, your creator, and He will give you the wisdom and tools to become your best, visible self. Live your truth out to the best of your ability.

Although the road to emerging out of invisibility into visibility can be long and treacherous, don't give up! You are worth the fight it takes to become that person you will love waking up to in the morning. As a matter of fact, be your own chief cheerleader and inspiration. Indeed, daily the power of choice is in your hands. It's up to you to decide what you will do with what life brings your way. Don't hand that power to anyone else.

Sometimes invisibility is created because of adversity. Adversity defined means hardship, difficulty, danger, and misfortunes. It comes in stages and in different seasons of your life and has different faces such as brokenness, humiliation, betrayal, abandonment, abuse, misuse, insults, false accusations, lies, and bullying. Regardless of how this invisibility factor shows up, use it to your advantage. The pain of adversity can strip away all that is superficial and artificial.

We have wasted too much of our lives trying to conform to other people's ideas and opinions. Frankly, that burden is too painful to carry, and the real you is crying out to be heard and seen. Let adversity cause you to grow up and discover the real you. Learn from it. The lyrics of a song asks, "Who are you? I really wanna know. Who are you? Tell me, who are you?" So I ask the question: Do you know who you are? You must answer that question yourself. The success of you emerging out of invisibility into visibility weighs on you being able to answer that question. It is critical that you understand and appreciate who you are with all your failures, successes, strengths, weaknesses, and idiosyncrasies.

Further, adversity is meant to be a catalyst that reveals the gifts that are hiding inside of you. It forces you to discover who you really are. By all means, let it cause you to create a life portfolio filled with your gifts, virtues, and contributions. This portfolio will demonstrate that you are a visible and powerful life contributor. Some of the gifts you bring to the table of life may be strength, faith, power, courage, organization, creativity, compassion, wisdom, excellence, resiliency, love, and persistence. Then you can add your academics contribution as well. Start with the internal, for they will sustain the external accomplishments.

On the other hand, if you don't use it to your advantage, adversity can create a coffin within you. This coffin can be a place where you allow your purpose, dreams, and destiny to die and be laid to rest. Don't let this happen!

Instead, let adversity become your launching pad, your springboard, your transportation that will hurl you towards fulfilling your destiny and make you the successful person you were born to be.

For that purpose, the stories I have shared were meant to serve as coaching sessions, providing insight, corporate advice, and plans of action. Hopefully, you have gained some positive skills to help you navigate successfully through corporate America. In addition, they were meant to be a prod to help move you along, so you won't allow yourself to stay stuck in despair or uncertainty.

Similarly there is a story that will be birthed out of you that will heal, restore, and rescue others out of their invisibility. The words of a song are being written within your soul, and words are waiting to be written to fill the pages of a best seller. As a writer, I have tried to glean from other authors the necessary ingredients to become an effective writer. One of my favorite authors, Ann Kiemel Anderson, wrote, "Many people Jesus has called to be experiential authors are those He believes He can trust with more than the average amount of heartache and human suffering. Otherwise, what is there to write about that will touch people with reality, heart, and genuine compassion?"

In essence, your painful experiences of invisibility have served a purpose. Much has been written in this book to testify to that fact. By all means, build upon what you have learned and create your greatest success story!

Most importantly, I trust you have felt the love, encouragement, and friendship extended to you. Without a doubt, you are not alone on this journey. See my smile and hear my motivational cheery voice speaking. Don't give up! When you least expect it, a brighter tomorrow will appear around the bend. You are a champion, my friend. Visibility is on the horizon. Embrace it fiercely!

About the Author

Gwendolyn J. Wheeler was born in Joliet, Illinois, but grew up in Lynn, Massachusetts. She attended the Lynn public schools and obtained higher education by completing various college courses, workshops, seminars, and on-the-job training in corporate America. Her experiences in corporate America developed and honed skills within her that she could never obtain anywhere else.

Every journey has a beginning. Too many people start out not knowing where they are going—no real purpose or dreams are in view. Sometimes a journey is created by a present need that we want to satisfy. For an eighteen-year-old senior in high school, her corporate journey began early because the money was limited in the Wheelers' household. Her father died when she was fifteen years old, and her mother's LPN salary was not enough to cover all the living expenses. She did her best, but Gwen wanted to be one less person her mother had to take care of. Financial independence was a priority for her even then.

Gwen started writing this book about her corporate journey in 2005 while she was still working. However, there were lessons she had learned that could not be publicly published then. After thirty-seven years of working in corporate America in various positions, she retired in January 2009. She finished her story. Putting the finishing touches on her portrait of thirty-seven years in corporate America was the goal of this book. This is her dramatic farewell.